Java in Telecommunications

WILEY SERIES IN COMMUNICATIONS NETWORKING & DISTRIBUTED SYSTEMS

Series Editor: David Hutchison, Lancaster University
Series Advisers: Harmen van As, TU Vienna
                 Serge Fdidia, University of Paris
                 Joe Sventek, Agilent Laboratories, Edinburgh

The 'Wiley Series in Communications Networking & Distributed Systems' is a series of expert-level, technically detailed books covering cutting-edge research and brand new developments in networking, middleware and software technologies for communications and distributed systems. The books will provide timely, accurate and reliable information about the state-of-the-art to researchers and development engineers in the telecommunications and computing sectors.

Other titles in the series:

Wright: *Voice over Packet Networks*
Sutton: *Secure Communications*

Java in Telecommunications
Solutions for Next Generation Networks

Thomas C. Jepsen, Editor
Programming Languages Editor
IT Professional Magazine

Farooq Anjum
Telcordia Technologies

Ravi Raj Bhat
Trillium Digital Systems, Inc.

Ravi Jain
Telcordia Technologies

Anirban Sharma
ONI Systems, Inc.

Douglas Tait
Sun Microsystems, Inc.

JOHN WILEY & SONS LTD

Chichester • New York • Weinheim • Brisbane • Singapore • Toronto

Other Wiley Editorial Offices

John Wiley & Sons, Inc., 605 Third Avenue,
New York, NY 10158-0012, USA

WILEY-VCH Verlag GmbH
Pappelallee 3, D-69469 Weinheim, Germany

John Wiley & Sons Australia, Ltd, 33 Park Road, Milton,
Queensland 4064, Australia

John Wiley & Sons (Canada) Ltd, 22 Worcester Road
Rexdale, Ontario, M9W 1L1, Canada

John Wiley & Sons (Asia) Pte Ltd, 2 Clementi Loop #02-01,
Jin Xing Distripark, Singapore 129809

Library of Congress Cataloguing-in-Publication Data
Java in telecommunications : solutions for next generatiion networks / Thomas C. Jepsen,
editor ; [contributions by] Farooq Anjum ... [et al.].
       p. cm.
    Includes bibliographical references and index.
    ISBN 0-471-49826-2 (alk.paper)
     1. Java (Computer program language) 2. Telecommunication systems. I. Jepsen,
Thomas C. II. Anjum, Farooq.

    QA76.73.J38 J368 2001
    005.13'3--dc21

                                                            2001026305

British Library Cataloguing in Publication Data

A catalogue record for this book is available from the British Library

ISBN 0 471 49826 2

Typeset in 10/12 pt Times by Deerpark Publishing Services Ltd, Shannon, Ireland

This book is printed on acid-free paper responsibly manufactured from sustainable forestry, in which at least two trees are planted for each one used for paper production.

Contents

Acknowledgements

The editors and authors would like to thank colleagues with whom they collaborated in writing articles on JAIN in the January 2000 issue of *IEEE Communications Magazine*: Rajeev Gupta, John de Keijzer, and Rob Goedman for allowing us to use some of the figures in those articles and their feedback on this section.

I would like to thank all the contributors for their hard work and diligence; I would also like to thank Brian Thorstad and Bryan Hendricks of Fujitsu Network Communications for their review comments and suggestions. And lastly, special thanks to our editors at Wiley, Sally Mortimore and Birgit Gruber, for bringing this project to a successful conclusion.

Thomas C. Jepsen, Editor

I would like to dedicate Chapter 2 to my wife Nandita Bhat for her constant support and inspiration while I was writing the text for this chapter.

Ravi Raj Bhat

1

Introduction

Thomas C. Jepsen

Programming Languages Editor, IT Professional, USA

1.1 Java in telecommunications

In the short span of 6 years of Java's commercial history, Java has shown itself to be a highly innovative and versatile programming language. Its platform independence, downloadability, and object oriented structure have made it the language of choice for a wide variety of business and scientific applications, and it is destined to play a leading role in the development of Internet-based electronic commerce systems.

Java's platform independence and mobility have also led to its wide use in telecommunications applications. The initial use for Java in telecommunications was in the development of write-once, run-anywhere graphical user interfaces for network and element management systems. Java now promises to become ubiquitous in the network; it is found in end-user applications, downloadable protocol support, call control applications, and open service creation environments.

The growing use of Java in telecommunications provides an opportunity to solve problems and meet challenges in the rapidly changing telecommunications environment of the new millennium:

- *Reducing the complexity of intelligent networks*. The close coupling between intelligent network applications and the call state machine in the present public switched telephone network (PSTN) results in complicated interactions among call processing features, and increases the complexity of new feature development. By providing a generic "middleware" layer for call/session control, Java allows decoupling of applications and state machines, and reduces feature interdependency.

- *Convergence of circuit (PSTN) and packet networks.* The rapid growth of the Internet, the widespread use of packet networks for transport of voice services, and the need to provide access to conventional PSTN telephony services via the Internet have created a need for interworking between networks. Java-based component software can provide the necessary platform-independent protocol support.

- *Integration of network management functions.* Integration of network management functions in converged networks increases operability and maintainability while providing economies of scale. Java's management-related packages allow integrated management capabilities to be put together in a building-block fashion.

- *Serving the needs of new service providers in an increasingly competitive environment.* Previously, telephony services were developed in a closed environment, using proprietary software and interfaces. Network convergence has created a need for an open service creation environment and mobile, platform-independent software. Java's standardized application programming interfaces (APIs) and built-in security features allow new service providers to create new and innovative services without proprietary restrictions.

1.2 California dreaming and the wizards of Menlo Park: a brief history of Java

Like the electric light and phonograph 100 years before, Java was dreamed up in truly Edisonian fashion in a place called Menlo Park by a bunch of eccentric experimenters who liked to take things apart. Java began in 1991 as a project codenamed "Green" at a Sun Microsystems facility in Menlo Park, California. The original idea was to develop software that would run on consumer electronics, rather than computers; to familiarize themselves with this novel environment, programmers James Gosling, Patrick Naughton, and Mike Sheridan began taking apart television sets and computer games, looking for interesting bits of hardware. To make this idea practical, however, required software that was not tied to a specific execution platform, but which could execute on any kind of hardware. For Gosling, a senior programmer at Sun and one of the project's leaders, the big conceptual breakthrough came when he attended a Doobie Brothers concert in nearby Mountain View, California. Looking up at the wires connecting the lights and the sound system, Gosling had a vision of "imaginary packets flowing down the wires making everything happen." (David Bank, "The Java Saga," Wired 3.12 (December 1995), 238.)

What Gosling had envisioned was the ability to create software functional units that could be downloaded and executed remotely. But no programming language then in existence supported this capability. The Green team quickly set to work to develop a new language, which Gosling called "Oak," that would support these capabilities.

The first attempt at a real-world application for Oak was a prototype set top box, built in 1993 for an interactive television network Time Warner was developing in Orlando, Florida. However, Sun lost the bid to Silicon Graphics, Inc., and the project entered a period of disarray. Unix guru Bill Joy and Sun's chief technology officer Eric Schmidt re-focused Oak to target the emerging Internet. The Internet itself was undergoing a revolutionary change, due to the development of the first graphically-based browser, Mosaic, by Marc Andreesen at the National Center for Supercomputing Applications in 1993.

The new language was re-named "Java" in January 1995, and the Internet turned out to be its "killer app." Java programs, in the form of *applets*, could be downloaded across the Internet to perform web browser functions that ranged from simple animation to complex business transactions. Sun created a subsidiary called Javasoft to develop and market the new language. Although Sun developed a completely Java-based browser called "Hotjava," the commercial success of the new language was assured when Netscape included Java support in their Navigator Browser late in 1995.

1.2.1 Reasons for Java's rapid rise in popularity and acceptance

From the beginning, Java programming tools were available to developers free of charge in the Java Developer's Kit (JDK), which could be downloaded over the Internet from the Sun website [1]. Java's developers, together with product manager Kim Polese, were influenced by both the success of the GNU free software movement and the emerging open source movement. They reasoned that making the software readily available was the best way to quickly create a market for Java applications and build a pool of Java-savvy developers.

Two primary reasons for Java's rapid acceptance are its architecture independence and its platform independence. Java programs are first compiled into an intermediate form called *bytecode*, which is interpreted at run time in a platform-specific *Java virtual machine*, or JVM. This approach allows Java programs to be written independently of the execution environment, and to execute in a nearly identical fashion in any Java-aware execution environment without the need for porting. Thus it is possible to download applets across the Internet to a wide variety of clients and have them execute the same function regardless of the supporting platform.

Another feature that boosted Java's popularity was its support of internationalization. Because of its support of the full Unicode standard, applications can be developed to support almost any language and character set, and can be easily converted from one language to another. This led to the adoption of Java by the international software community, and to the early availability of non-English versions of the JDK.

From the beginning, Java has been blessed with quality documentation, and this has been another big factor in its success. Too many programming languages have suffered from mediocre or incomplete documentation; this in turn has led to a "tree-house" mentality in which novice programmers gain entrance into the private clubhouse of the elite by learning the undocumented secrets of the language

Perhaps the most important reason for the rapid adoption of Java is that programmers like to use it. Java is a hands-on language; it was never intended to be the sort of academic language that generates more Ph.D. dissertations than debugged executables. Rather, to use James Gosling's expression, Java was designed to be a "blue collar language" and a "language for a job." (James Gosling, "The Feel of Java," IEEE Computer (June 1997), 53.)

1.2.2 Real-world uses for Java

As mentioned before, the development of the graphically-based World Wide Web was the "killer application" that created the initial interest in Java. The increasing number of electronic commerce (e-commerce) applications has contributed to the ongoing use of Java for graphical user interfaces (GUIs), mobile agents, and server-side functions (servlets). Java's built-in security features make it well-suited for e-commerce applications.

Business applications use Java to migrate programs from mainframes to client–server environments, and to update legacy software by providing structured, object-oriented versions of programs originally written in report program generator (RPG) or COBOL. By adding a layer of common business objects between the application-specific business processes and the virtual machine, applications can be converted rapidly and efficiently.

Java has found wide use in telecommunications applications. Java has been used to develop telecommunications management network (TMN)-based network management systems using CORBA distributed object technology; a CORBA interface is now a part of the standard set of Java packages. The Java APIs for integrated networks (JAIN™) community has begun development of a comprehensive set of applications and protocols for intelligent networking, and an open service creation environment for developing new network applications. And Java is likely to play a leading role in the development of set top box applications for residential broadband services.

Reliability is a primary requirement of telecommunications applications. Java's use of a virtual machine and automated garbage collection largely eliminates the possibility of buffer overflow due to programming errors, enhancing its reliability.

1.2.3 Java applets and applications

There are two basic types of Java programs: applets and applications. Java applications are similar to applications written in other languages. They contain a `main()` method, variable declarations, and executable statements. Java applications are compiled into bytecode, which is then interpreted at runtime. Java provides platform independence by means of a *virtual machine*, which isolates the bytecode from the details of the platform on which it is executing. Thus bytecode written on any platform will execute in a nearly identical manner on any other platform which supports a Java virtual machine. (The notion of using a virtual machine to provide platform independence is not original to Java; both Smalltalk and Pascal have used a similar virtual machine approach to platform independence.)

Applets, on the other hand, are portable units of code that do not have a `main()` method. Applets are intended to execute remotely from where they were created, typically in a web browser environment. References to Java applets are embedded in hypertext markup language (HTML) by means of an `<APPLET>` tag. The uniform resource locator (URL) specifying the location of the applet is given in a *codebase* parameter. When the HTML is executed, the applet is downloaded from the URL and executed in the Java runtime environment provided by the browser.

For security reasons, applets are normally given only limited access to resources in the local execution environment. Untrusted applets (i.e. applets downloaded over the Internet with no special security privileges) are not allowed to read, write, rename, or delete files on the local system. They are not allowed to create network connections to any computer other than the one from which they were downloaded; and they are not allowed to invoke any program on the local system.

1.2.4 The JDK

The JDK is a downloadable software package that provides programmers with the tools necessary to begin developing applications in Java. The JDK includes the *appletviewer*, which downloads and displays all applets referenced in a specified HTML document; *java*, the Java bytecode interpreter used to run Java applications; *jre*, a runtime interpreter similar to java but intended for users who do not need development-related options; *javac*, the Java compiler, which is used to compile Java source code into bytecodes; *javadoc*, the Java documentation generator for creating class documentation files; *javah*, which generates header files for writing native methods in C or C++; *javap*, the class disassembler, which disassembles class files and prints out public fields, methods, and constructors; and *jdb*, a text-based, command-line debugger for Java classes.

Recent versions of the JDK also include tools for remote method invocation (RMI) application development; internationalization tools for converting non-Unicode files to Unicode format; a *jar* tool for combining multiple class files into a single

Java archive (JAR) file; and a *javakey* tool for generating digital signatures for archive files.

The JDK also serves as a mechanism for releasing changes and new features. The original JDK 1.0, released in late 1995, provided a minimal set of functions. JDK 1.1 was released in early 1997; it included signed applets for security, object serialization, and the Remote Method Interface as new features, as well as enhancements to the existing graphics, networking, and I/O capabilities. JDK 1.2, released in late 1998, included a CORBA interface and an improved security model; it has now been upgraded to a full release, and is referred to as the Software Developers' Kit (SDK), Release 2.

1.2.5 Java packages and classes

Java as an object-oriented language, consists of *classes*, which in turn consist of data and the methods that operate on the data. Data is present in classes in the form of fields; the visibility of these fields to other classes and applications can be specified as *public*, *private*, or *protected*. As in other object-oriented languages, a program must create an *instance* of a class (that is, define a specific example of the class and allocate resources to it) to do useful work.

The Java class library is composed of a set of *packages,* which are java classes organized according to function and purpose. Thus the java.applet package consists of classes for creating applets, and java.io consists of classes for performing input/ output operations. Packages are made available to classes by means of an import statement placed at the beginning of a Java program. For example, placing the statement

```
import java.io.*;
```

at the beginning of a java program makes all classes belonging to the package java.io available to the classes in the program. (The java.lang core package is imported by default in all java programs and does not need to be explicitly declared.)

1.2.6 The original core Java packages

The core Java functionality is provided by about half a dozen packages, which have been part of the JDK since the beginning. The java.applet package contains the classes used to create applets, small programs that execute in a web browser or other application. All applets are subclasses of the **java.applet.Applet** class. The java.applet package is itself a subclass of the java.awt (abstract windowing toolkit) package.

The java.awt package provides capabilities for visual display, including graphics, windowing components, and layout managers. Important classes include **java.awt.Graphics**, which includes methods for drawing lines and shapes;

java.awt.Component, which is the superclass of all GUI components, such as buttons, lists, windows, and panels; and **java.awt.LayoutManager**, which enables components to be manipulated within a container object.

It is possible to create a simple "hello world" applet with just the applet package and the awt package; for example,

```
import java.applet.*;
import java.awt.*;

public class HelloWorld extends Applet {
  public void paint (Graphics g) {
    g.drawString("Hello World", 50, 50);
  }
}
```

In this simple program, a **HelloWorld** class is created which inherits the behavior of **java.applet.Applet**, and is therefore an applet itself. A `paint()` method is invoked on a **java.awt.Graphics** object **g**, which uses the `drawString` method to draw a text string, "Hello World," at the specified location in the window created by the appletviewer or browser that displays the applet. If this Java source code is placed in a file called HelloWorld.java and compiled using javac, a class file called **HelloWorld.class** will be created. To display the applet, it must be embedded in HTML text using something like the following:

```
<HTML>
<HEAD>
  <TITLE>First Hello Applet</TITLE>
</HEAD>
<BODY>
  <P>"Hello World applet..."
  <APPLET>
  code = "HelloWorld.class" width = 400 height = 300>
  </APPLET>
</BODY>
</HTML>
```

A user can view the applet using a Java-enabled browser or the Java applet viewer.

Another basic Java package is the java.io package, which provides a Java program with the ability to read data from a variety of sources, and to write data to a corresponding variety of sinks. The two basic classes are **java.io.InputStream** and **java.io.OutputStream**, which are the superclasses of all I/O streams. Some common I/O functions include **FileInputStream**, which allows data to be read from a file; **BufferedInputStream**, which allows read data to be buffered; and **FilterOutputStream**, which allows the data written to an **OutputStream** to be filtered.

The java.lang package is the core package that provides the basic functionality of the Java programming language. It provides class wrappers for primitive data types, including booleans, characters, and integers. It provides classes to represent strings, which are immutable once created, and string buffers, which can be modified after creation. It provides a **system** class to interface with system functions in a platform-independent manner, and a **thread** class to create control threads on the Java interpreter. It also provides the **throwable** class, which is the root class for java exception handling.

The java.net package contains the classes that provide networking capability. A **URL** class represents a Uniform Resource Locator, and enables objects to be downloaded from the URL or streams to be set up to read from or write to the specified URL. **Socket** and **ServerSocket** classes enable TCP/IP client–server networking, and an **InetAddress** class allows an Internet address to be specified.

The java.util package contains classes that perform a variety of "utility-like" functions, including a **date** class, a **hashtable** class, and a class which implements a pseudo-random number generator.

1.2.7 Additions to the Java packages

The modular structure of Java's packages makes it possible to add new functionality in an incremental fashion, allowing the language to continue to evolve in response to user requirements and technology development. The following section describes some of the functions that have been added or modified since the original release of Java.

Security

The initial security model for Java was the *sandbox* model, in which local code was considered to be trusted and had full access to resources, while applets downloaded from remote sites were considered to be untrusted code. Untrusted applets were confined to the "sandbox," where they had no access to local resources, such as file access and program execution. JDK1.1 added the java.security package, which permitted the creation and verification of *signed applets*. Signed applets have a signature which is created using a private key; they can be verified using a public key and given trusted access to local resources.

SDK 2 introduced a fine-grained security policy that enables individual Java applets and applications to be given permissions to use specified resources. This was a refinement of the previous (coarse-grained) approach, where applets had either total access or no access to local resources. Access to a specific file or port would be given only to programs that needed it.

Java database connectivity (JDBC)

JDBC is provided by the java.sql package added in JDK1.1. JDBC provides a standard query language (SQL) database interface, allowing access to a wide variety of relational databases. It includes an object database connectivity (ODBC) bridge, which is an ODBC-standard C API.

Java native interface

There are cases where it is desirable to interface code written in other languages to Java. For example, if a large amount of functional code already exists, it may be more economical to simply adapt it to interact with newly developed Java programs. Or it may be necessary to use native code to perform system-specific or time-critical functions. The Java native interface (JNI) provides a standard programming interface for writing *native methods* to accomplish these functions.

JavaBeans

The java.beans package added in JDK1.1 supports JavaBeans, java classes that can be manipulated in a visual builder tool and combined into GUI applications. Java-Beans are components with standard property and event interface conventions; they can interoperate with ActiveX and OpenDoc components. JavaBeans have a separate Beans Development Kit (BDK), which includes a BeanBox sample container for testing JavaBeans.

Remote method invocation

The java.rmi package added in JDK1.1 supports remote method invocation, or RMI. RMI enables distributed Java-to-Java applications, in which the methods of remote Java objects can be invoked from other Java virtual machines on different hosts. A Java program can make a call on a remote object once it obtains a reference to the remote object, either by looking up the remote object in the bootstrap-naming service provided by RMI, or by receiving the reference as an argument or return value.

The Java 2 Enterprise Edition SDK supports the transport of RMI requests over the CORBA Internet Inter-ORB protocol, thus making RMI compatible with the Object Management Group's CORBA specifications.

Java IDL

The Java IDL package, first included in SDK 2, adds CORBA capability to the Java platform, enabling web-based Java applications to transparently invoke operations on remote network services using the industry-standard Object Management Group (OMG) Interface Definition Language (IDL) and Internet Inter-ORB Protocol

(IIOP). (While RMI provides similar functionality in a pure Java environment, the CORBA IDL allows Java applications to access distributed objects written in other languages, such as C or C++.)

Java foundation classes

The Java foundation classes (JFC) added to SDK 2 extend the functionality of the **java.awt** classes by adding a comprehensive set of GUI class libraries. The primary content of the JFC are the swing classes, which provide pluggable look-and-feel capability and allow users to switch the look and feel of an application without restarting it. The swing capability allows developers to either create a generic cross-platform look-and-feel, which looks the same on all platforms, or to default to the look-and-feel of the specific platform on which the application is executing.

Enterprise JavaBeans, Servlets, and JSPs

The Enterprise Edition of the Java 2 platform supports a number of new server-oriented features intended for use in a multi-tier, thin-client environment, including Enterprise JavaBeans, Servlets, and Java server pages (JSPs). Online applications have evolved from the original client–server, or two-tiered, model, to a multi-tiered model in which layers of business logic and middleware separate traditional server functions from client requests. Clients have evolved toward a "thin" model in which most of the application functionality has migrated to the server side, and updates to the user interface are provided by serving HTML or extensible markup language (XML) pages to the client in an interactive fashion.

Enterprise JavaBeans, like ordinary JavaBeans, are java-based component software; however, Enterprise JavaBeans are used to provide server-side business logic or middleware functions, while JavaBeans are used to implement client-side GUIs. Servlets are applet-like components that provide CGI-like functions on the server, providing an interface between client requests and system services, without the performance limitations inherent in CGI scripts. While CGI scripts must start a new process for each new request, servlets execute in a virtual machine that runs in the same process space as the server, thus minimizing overheads. Servlets can also use the JDBC API to provide direct access to databases.

JSPs are used to interactively update client user interfaces. JSPs use XML- or HTML-like tags and Java *scriptlets* to encapsulate the logic that generates the content for the page. This allows most of the application logic to remain on the server and to send responses back to the client in the form of HTML or XML pages. A simple example of a JSP is a function to return the date and time to a client:

```
<HTML>
<HEAD>
  <TITLE>Date and Time</TITLE>
</HEAD>
<BODY>
  The date and time:
  <% = new Date()%>.
</BODY>
</HTML>
```

JSP allows any legal Java expression to be placed between the % markers. Thus when the above JSP is requested by a client, the `Java Date()` method returns a date and time which is contained in the HTML returned to the client [2].

Realtime Java

Realtime applications require that functions execute within predefined time constraints. This in turn requires control over memory management and resource allocation. Applications in robotics, telecommunications switching, and multimedia typically use realtime capabilities. In order to support development of realtime applications, functional extensions to the Java language are required. A *Real Time Specification for Java* has been developed and released by the Java Community Process (JCP) to define and document the required extensions [3].

Java for Linux

The tremendous interest generated by the Linux operating system has created a demand for Linux versions of Java among developers who wish to exploit the synergy between the two technologies. Linux enthusiasts have used the JDK for Linux created by the Blackdown Project for years [4]. Sun Microsystems has now announced its own version of the Java 2 SDK for Linux, which includes an x86 JIT compiler [5].

Java and XML

XML has also created much interest among Java developers. XML's extensible data types fit well with Java's platform independent executables, and combining the two provides interoperability and scaleability for application-to-application messaging. Many Java-based tools for generating and processing XML have been developed. The World Wide Web Consortium's Document Object Model specification for XML contains a Java language binding [6].

1.2.8 Looking toward the future

Clearly, Java is here to stay. Indeed, with its proven ability to evolve at warp speed and keep up with the Internet's rapid growth, Java's future looks promising. Some likely evolutionary paths for Java include performance improvement, mobile agents, and distributed computing.

Performance improvements

While the virtual machine approach enables platform independence, it also adds an extra layer to the runtime environment. The developers of Java have worked to enhance the performance of the Java virtual machine through optimized bytecode execution, faster memory allocation, and an improved garbage collector algorithm. As a result, the runtime performance of many Java applications now compares favorably with identical implementations written in native languages. Another approach is to provide a just-in-time compiler (JIT) to convert bytecodes to optimized native object code for a specific execution environment.

Mobile agents

e-Commerce applications will require mobile agents that can move through the network, interact with their environment intelligently, and negotiate on behalf of their clients. Java is the language of choice for implementing mobile agents. Java's support of object serialization allows agents (and their state) to be transformed into a format suitable for transport through a network and reconstructed in a remote location [7].

Distributed computing and networking

Java is well-suited for distributed computing applications, due to its mobility and platform independence. Scientific applications use Java to breakdown complex problem spaces into individual executables that can be downloaded to a large number of execution platforms, making it possible to use the Internet for high-performance computing. Jini, a recently developed Java-based networking application, allows impromptu networking of computers, appliances, and home entertainment devices through a simple *discovery and join* process. Devices and services can register with the network, and users can find them by using a lookup service [8]. Another recent Java initiative is JXTA, short for "juxtapose," which proposes the use of Java for distributed peer-to-peer computing.

1.3 Organization of this book

This book is divided into seven chapters. Each chapter discusses a different Java application for telecommunications, and provides a unique perspective on using Java to solve telecommunications-related problems.

Chapter 1, *Introduction*, by Thomas C. Jepsen, provides background on how the Java language was developed, and discusses the functional capabilities of the language. It also provides an overview of the organization of the book and the content of each section.

Chapter 2, *Java APIs for Integrated Networks*, by Ravi Raj Bhat of Trillium Systems and Douglas Tait of Sun Microsystems, describes the Java APIs for integrated networks, or JAIN technology. It covers JAIN architecture, protocol APIs, and JAIN in converged (PSTN/Internet) networks. It also provides an overview of the Java Community Process and the JAIN Protocol Experts Group.

Chapter 3, *Java Call Control*, by Farooq Anjum and Ravi Jain of Telcordia Technologies, defines an API for Java call control (JCC). The JCC API defines the interface for applications to initiate and manipulate calls.

Chapter 4, *Realtime Java for Telecommunications*, by Thomas C. Jepsen, provides an overview of the extensions required to do realtime programming using Java. It also discusses the *Realtime Specification for Java*, developed by the realtime Java Experts Working Group as part of the Java Community Process.

Chapter 5, *Network Management Using Java*, by Anirban Sharma of ONI Systems, discusses Java tools and technologies for developing network management applications based on the Telecommunications Management Network (TMN) model. It includes an example application using servlets and EJBs.

Chapter 6, *XML and Java for Telecommunications*, by Thomas C. Jepsen, discusses XML and its relationship to telecommunications and electronic business XML (ebXML). It describes the telecommunications-related XML standards being defined by the World Wide Web Consortium (W3C), OASIS/CEFACT, and ATIS/T1M1, and discusses the Java tools that have been developed by the JCP for XML.

Formatting conventions

In the following sections, Java classes and objects will be printed in bold type. Java methods will be printed in Arial typeface, and Java interfaces will appear in italics.

References

1. Java Home Page, http://java.sun.com.
2. For a good overview of JSPs, see Brown K, Craig G. Using Java server pages – servlets made simple. Java Report August 1999;41–50.
3. Bollella G, Brosgol B, Dibble P, Furr S, Gosling J, Hardin D, Turnbull M. The Realtime Specification for Java, http://java.sun.com/aboutJava/communityprocess/first/jsr001/index.html.
4. The Blackdown Project, http://www.blackdown.org.
5. SDK 2 for Linux, http://java.sun.com/j2se/1.3/download-linux.html.

6. Wood L, Apparao V, Byrne S, Champion MJ, Isaacs S, Jacobs I, Le Hors A, Nicol G, Robie J, Sutor R, Wilson C, editors. Document Object Model (DOM) Level 1 Specification Version 1.0 W3C Recommendation, 1 October 1998. http://www.w3.org/TR/1998/REC-DOM-Level-1-19981001.

7. Wong D et. al. Java-based mobile agents, Communications of the ACMMarch 1999;92–102.

8. JINI, http://java.sun.com/products/jini.

Portions of this chapter first appeared in the January issue of *IEEE Communications* © 2000 and the March/April edition of the IEEE's *IT Professional* © 2000. Both are reproduced with permission of the IEEE and are modified from the original text.

2

JAVA APIs for integrated networks

Ravi Raj Bhat
Trillium Systems, USA

and

Douglas Tait
Sun Microsystems, USA

2.1 The JAIN value proposition

We can enable next generation services and yet keep networks simple and scalable by making networking devices "intelligent-on-demand". The raw processing power of networking devices is at the highest level and Moore's law has never been better exemplified in the improvements made in the processing power of these devices. However, increasing the processing power of a networking device adds only muscle to it. To get better and efficient performance from the network we have to add intelligence in addition to the muscle to these networking devices. By strongly cohering high octane processing power with software intelligence optimized for the underlying processing platform, we can introduce certain intelligent devices into the network, which would act as proxies to other networking devices. However, increasing the number of devices to keep up with the demand for bandwidth and communication makes it difficult to centrally manage and coordinate the flow of information among the sea of networking devices. A solution for this problem is to decentralize and allow networking devices to be intelligent and self-sufficient. However, if intelligence is embedded in all networking devices at all times, we will defeat our initial goal of making networks simple and scalable. Therefore, a better solution is to provide the intelligence to the networking devices, as and when they need it, or in other words, make these devices "intelligent-on-demand". This requires dynamic software loading and execution. Java computing is an ideal candidate to provide such a capability.

Before we go out and replace the software in existing networking devices to run in Java, we have to think about the economics of doing so. A huge amount of investment has gone into the existing network infrastructure and it would be prohibitively expensive to replace all the software in this device with Java. Therefore, we have to follow an evolutionary path rather than a revolutionary path. The Java APIs for integrated networks (JAIN) technology provides an elegant solution for this problem. JAIN API is a set of integrated network APIs for the Javα™ platform, provides a framework to build and integrate solutions (or "services") that span across packet (e.g. Internet Protocol (IP) or Asynchronous Transfer Mode (ATM)), wireless, and PSTN networks. The objective of JAIN API is to provide service portability, convergence, and secure access (by services residing outside of the network) to such integrated networks. The JAIN API is defined and specified by a large number of participating communication companies (the JAIN Community), and according to a well-documented process known as the Java Community Process[SM] (abbreviated as JCP). The goals of JCP are listed in the text inset. For further details on JCP please refer to [16]. The objective of the JAIN Community is to create an open market for services across integrated networks using Java technology.

JAIN technology builds on Java portability by standardizing the information flow, in the form of API, to and from the signaling layer of the communications networks into the Java language, and defines a communications framework for services to be created, tested, and deployed over this API. The strengths of JAIN technology are in service portability, network convergence, and secure network access:

- *Service portability*: technology and application development are currently constrained by proprietary interfaces. Portability of applications is almost non-existent. This increases application development cost, time to market, and maintenance requirements. The JAIN approach is to reshape proprietary interfaces into uniform Java interfaces delivering portable applications.

- *Network convergence*: call or session legs for most of today's applications and services typically span only a single type of network – public switched telephone network (PSTN), packet, or wireless – although clearly gateways between these networks do exist. The higher-level (discussed later) JAIN call models include facilities for observing, initiating, answering, processing, and manipulating calls, where a call is understood to include a multimedia, multiparty, multi-protocol session over the underlying integrated network.

Sun Microsystems, Inc., introduced the Java Community Process^{SM} program on December 8, 1998, for the development and revision of Java technology specifications. The goals (sourced from http://java.sun.com/aboutJava/community-process/background.html) of the Java Community Process^{SM} program are to:

- Enable the broader Java Community to participate in the proposal, selection, and development of Java APIs by establishing a means for both licensees and non-licensees to participate.

- Enable members of the Java Community to propose and carry out new API development efforts without the need for Sun engineers to be actively involved.

- Ensure that the process is faithfully followed by all participants each time it is used by enabling auditing at key milestones.

- Ensure that each specification is backed by both a reference implementation and the associated suite of conformance tests.

- Help foster a good liaison between the Java Community and other bodies such as consortia, standards bodies, academic research groups, and non-profit organizations.

- *Secure network access*: communication applications and services run either inside the operator's trusted network or completely outside this network. The JAIN Service Provider API interface enables untrusted services, residing outside the network, to directly access network resources to carry out specifications or functions inside the integrated network.

JAIN technology creates a new environment for developers and users of communication services to build systems on a set of standards guaranteed to run on conformant networks. The market opportunity for new services in such an environment has Internet-like growth potential. Merging the rapid service creation and deployment model in the Internet space and the proven quality of service of the PSTN creates a new market scenario. JAIN technology further enhances the convergence of the Internet and PSTN by providing controlled access of untrusted services to the available functionality and intelligence inside the networks. Parlay (and JAIN Service Provider API) services become network-operator-independent, making it attractive to develop interesting services by service providers and third parties. The focus of the JAIN effort is to take the telecommunications market from many proprietary systems to a single open, distributed environment, not unlike the Internet today, able to host a large variety of services while still maintaining quality and reliability of service. By opening the network to Java applications, an opportunity is created to deliver thousands of portable, integrated services rather than the dozens currently available.

JAIN technology is based on Java component (bean) technology: components can be added, taken away, enhanced, assembled, shared, or redistributed (even geographically) in a dynamic running system. This allows services and features to be added, updated, and deleted in a live environment. The removal of proprietary interfaces opens markets where network equipment providers (NEPs), independent software vendors (ISVs), protocol stack vendors, service providers, and carriers will be able to build and sell a variety of Java-technology-adapted components. Service providers and NEPs will then be able to select "best of breed" JAIN-conformant products from different vendors on the basis of functionality and value.

What is a component model?

A (software) component model is a set of principles that define how solutions can be built from smaller (software) entities. The component model builds on the concept of components and containers. Components (also known as objects) are reusable software building blocks with encapsulated application code and associated data structures. Components execute within a construct called a container. A container provides an application context for one or more components and provides management and control services for the components. In practical terms, a container provides an operating system process or thread in which to execute the component. Components are usually classified into two types: client and server. Client components normally execute within some type of visual container, such as a web page. Server components are non-visual and execute within a container that is provided by an application server, such as a web server.

In the Java component model constructs are known as beans, and examples of currently available beans are JavaBeans, Enterprise JavaBeans, Federated Beans, and MBeans. Here they are referred to as *-Beans. The principles cover many aspects of the entire lifecycle of the *-Beans, such as

- how individual beans can be assembled into larger entities and ultimately into complete solutions
- how entities are visible in development tools
- how *-Beans are deployed when they are needed in a running system
- how many instances are needed to obtain the right level of performance
- whether the *-Beans are location-independent (in a local network or even in a wide-area network)

This *open value chain* market model stimulates the reuse of existing components and the development of additional or missing functionality – maximizing efficiency as well as innovation. It also opens the market to innovative new players. The next-generation architecture provided by JAIN APIs creates a level playing field for deploying new services. This model is best served when all levels of the communications industry participate: hardware companies, stack providers, NEPs, and network and service providers

2.2 JAIN architecture

The JAIN architecture comprises a set of integrated network APIs for the Java platform and an environment to build and integrate JAIN components into services or applications that work across PSTN, packet (e.g. IP or asynchronous transfer mode, ATM), and wireless networks. The JAIN approach integrates wireline, wireless, and packet-based networks by separating service-based logic from network-based logic. Thus, from this point of view, tye JAIN architecture consists of two layers, application and protocol. This is illustrated in Figure 2.1.

- The protocol layer in the JAIN architecture standardizes interfaces to IP, wireline, and wireless signaling protocols. These protocols include TCAP, ISUP, INAP, MAP, SIP, MGCP, Megaco, and H.323.

- The application layer in the JAIN architecture defines service provider APIs (JAIN SPA) based on the specifications from the Parlay group (www.

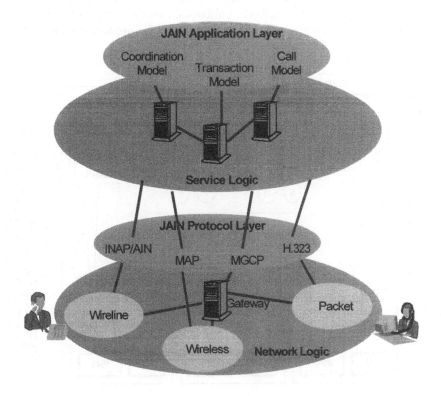

Figure 2.1 *Layered approach for JAIN (sourced from [7]).*

parlay.org), Java call control (JCC), and a JAIN service creation environments (JAIN SCE), and carrier grade JAIN service logic execution environment (JAIN SLEE).

The protocol layer in the JAIN architecture is based on Java standardization of specific protocols (SIP, MGCP, H.323, TCAP, ISUP, INAP/AIN, MAP, etc.). By providing standardized protocol interfaces in a Java object model, applications and protocol stacks can be dynamically interchanged and, at the same time, provide a high degree of portability to the applications in the application layer using protocol stacks from different vendors. Section 2.3 explains the JAIN protocol APIs in detail.

The application layer in the JAIN architecture provides a generic call (or session) model across heterogeneous networks. The fundamental idea is to provide a single interface from the service domain into the network(s). The application layer in the JAIN architecture also supports secure access to network resources accessible through JAIN APIs (i.e. the application layer call model or the individual protocols) using a set of packages and extensions known as JAIN SPA, which is an effort to incorporate Parlay APIs into the JAIN environment.

Figure 2.2 illustrates the three basic abstractions supported by the JAIN architecture. An application or service at the protocol level can talk directly to the *JAIN adapters*, which are Java class methods, callbacks, events, or Java interfaces that encapsulate the underlying resources. The resources may be implemented in Java, C, C++, and

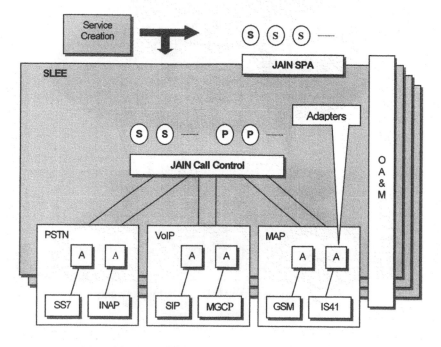

Figure 2.2   *JAIN abstractions (sourced from [7]).*

so on, but a JAIN-conformant protocol product does provide at least the relevant JAIN Java API. This lowest level of the JAIN abstraction does not provide any features to the application for dealing with different kinds of protocols; for example, an application that needs a session spanning INAP and SIP will have to handle both protocols. But it does provide for the same application to run on top of protocol products from different vendors.

A service or application at the next level of JAIN abstraction, the *Java call control* level in Figure 2.2. does not have to be aware that some of its session or call legs are using a different protocol. The JAIN architecture provides a third level of abstraction through *JAIN SPA*. In Figure 2.2, the little circles outside the SLEE box represent JAIN-SPA-based services. These are untrusted services and are also illustrated in Figure 2.3. JAIN SPA acts as a firewall to protect the security and integrity of the integrated network. Some operators might opt to have all services, both inside and outside their integrated network domain, use the JAIN SPA interface. The JAIN SPA interface exports some or all capabilities available inside the integrated network to services running inside a different security domain. A detailed description of JAIN SPA can be found in another section of this book (see also http://www.parlay.org).

Examples of capabilities addressed by JAIN SPA are a secure framework, JAIN JCC mobility features, a discovery service, and so forth. Figure 2.2 also shows the vertical bar labeled OA&M. These are a set of APIs that will provide for operational, administrative, and maintenance aspects of a JAIN environment.

2.2.1 JAIN service logic execution environment (JSLEE)

In Figures 2.2 and 2.3 the little circles inside the SLEE labeled S (for service) are the JAIN SLEE components. Services can be written directly on top of the JAIN protocol layer adapter APIs, JCC API, or JAIN SPA. This will facilitate portability of these services. Services will require and use much more than just a call model, though; for example, they might want to use Java's JDBC, text-to-speech, and JNDI APIs, to mention a few. Furthermore, JAIN's SLEE provides portable support for transactions, persistence, load balancing, security, object and connection instance pooling, and so on. The JSC and SLEE focus on a component model (see the box titled "What Is a Component Model?") over specific implementations. Enterprise JavaBeans (EJBs) (see the box on "The EJB Component Model") are an excellent candidate for such a component model [10], but it is certainly possible to use other component models, such as Jinι™ [11], Jini JavaSpaces [12], Jiro™ [13], or JES [14]. Most of these container structures, extended with the right features, are viable implementation platforms for JAIN SLEE. Figure 2.4 gives an example of a possible environment for an EJB-based JAIN implementation. In Figure 2.4 the application server provides one or more types of containers for different types of EJBs. The EJBs are the building blocks for services. An implementation of JAIN SLEE can be considered as an integrated network application server. The component model as

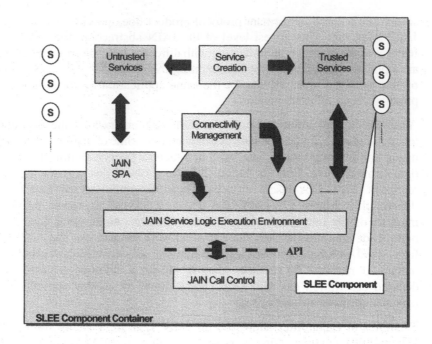

Figure 2.3 *JAIN service logic execution environment.*

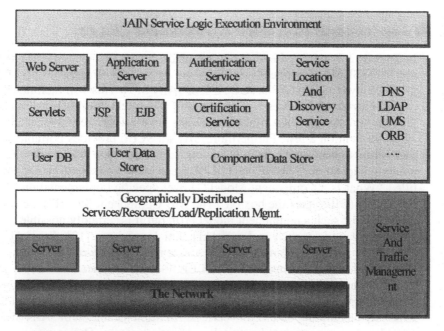

Figure 2.4 *Example of EJB-based JAIN implementation (sourced from [7]).*

defined for the SLEE also supports distributed implementations where portions of the SLEE are migrated to the edge of the network, say, to run on a residential gateway or even inside a consumer device.

2.3 JAIN protocol APIs

2.3.1 JAIN SS7 APIs

The JAIN Protocol APIs define interfaces for communications protocols used in telephony, intelligent networks (IN), wireless networks and the Internet. Protocol APIs are organized into signaling system no. 7 (SS7) APIs and Internet protocol (IP) APIs. In addition to the APIs, each JAIN protocol has an associated reference implementation (RI) and a technology compatibility kit (TCK). The RI is used to promote users for the API. The TCK is a suite of tests that a vendor must run and pass in order to claim JAIN compliance.

The EJB component model

The best known *-Beans are JavaBeans and EJBs. In the management domain MBeans have been around for several years. JavaBeans was the first software component model added to the Java world, and its primary focus was on reusable components, components that can be visually manipulated and customized in GUI development environments to assemble applications using introspection and a runtime event model to provide notification and callbacks.

Enterprise JavaBeans are focused on the enterprise problem domain. They deliver a server side software component model that supports the typical requirements of a database/transaction environment, such as access control, CORBA interoperability, object transaction monitors, availability, and load balancing. Each EJB does not provide all these facilities by itself; it relies on a so-called container for these services. This is exactly the strength of a *-Bean/container model: The developer of the *-Bean can focus on expressing the service logic without having to worry about usually complicated system-level issues (e.g. related to high availability and load balancing).

One of the differences between JavaBeans and EJBs is that JavaBeans can execute directly on the Java virtual machine. EJBs need a container to live in. In many cases it is attractive, though, to provide a container or agent for Java-Beans as well (e.g. to handle lifecycle issues or translate JavaBean events into some other event mechanism such as SNMP traps). This is the case in Java Management Extension (JMX), and the currently available reference implementation of JMX (see the box "What is JMX").

Most protocol software is written in native programming languages, such as C or assembly in order to increase performance. However, writing services in native languages, such as C, hinders fast and easy introduction of new services into networks. Programs written in native languages cannot be easily uploaded to a running system without retesting, relinking, and redeploying, all of which is very costly. Moreover, to dynamically upload the programs written in native languages, they have to be compiled to a target machine, thus requiring us to have some knowledge about the target machine. This slows down the process of dynamic software upload. Java, as an object-oriented programming language inherently supporting distributed, platform-independent computing, provides the framework to easily upload new objects for implementing various service components into the existing infrastructure. In order to utilize Java technology for this purpose, new service applications written in Java must be adapted to communicate with protocol layers that are implemented in native programming languages, such as C. The JAIN protocol APIs is an effort towards providing such an adaptation tool.

Due to various market forces and regional requirements, present telecommunication networks embody a myriad of "variants" for each protocol layer. Whenever a new protocol variant is introduced into the network to provide a new bearer service or some other advanced network-level service, application-level software entities must be upgraded to work with new protocol variants. The JAIN SS7 API is an attempt to abstract the network-level functionality from the idiosyncrasies of different protocol variants; such that changes in the underlying networks are transparent to the application. For example, in Figure 2.7, if we introduce JAIN ISUP and JAIN INAP API immediately above INAP and ISUP protocols and have the Service Location Protocol (SLP) and Basic Call Process (BCP) written in Java, we can dynamically upgrade the SLP and BCP logics remotely without ever bringing down the SSP or SCP. Figure 2.15 takes this concept further and illustrates an example of how JAIN APIs will fit into the current network to create a flexible future network.

At its core, the JAIN architecture defines a set of software components that enable an application, such as the service execution environment in an SCP or application server, or call control in SSP or Softswitch, executing in the Java space to access services provided by underlying protocol layers written in a native programming language. Network service components, known in IN as SIBs, are analogous to objects, or JavaBeans™ [6]. The service creation and management center shown in Figure 2.15 will create and upgrade the SIBs (illustrated in Figure 2.10) in Java and upload them at the service execution environment in real-time using either JMX or EJB environments. In addition, the JAIN SS7 API provides an operation, administration, and maintenance (OAM) API which is used to provision and acquire network specific data.

The software components defined in the JAIN APIs are based on the JavaBeans design pattern. Each JAIN protocol API defines three major Java software components: *Stack*, *Provider* and *Listener*. These three software components are defined in the form of Java interfaces (see Figure 2.5). The *Stack* component abstracts the

What is JMX?

JMX is an effort under the JCP to define appropriate management extensions for the Java platform. JMX provides

- an instrumentation level for control of elements (both software and hardware),
- an agent layer to group instrumentation level management entities,
- a manager layer to ease and consolidate distributed agents, and
- interfaces to management applications (including SNMP and TMN-based approaches).

A JMX manageable resource is one that has been instrumented in accordance with the JMX instrumentation level specification. It can be a business application, a device, or the software implementation of a service or policy. A managed bean, MBean for short, is a Java object that represents a JMX manageable resource. MBeans follow the JavaBean™ component model (see the box "What is a component model?") closely. A JMX agent is an Mbean server/ container. It will have at least one connector or adaptor to communicate (e.g. using HTTP, RMI, or SNMP) and may contain one or more management services, also represented as MBeans. The MBean server is a registry for MBeans in the agent and also allows for manipulation of those MBeans. The JMX manager provides one or more interfaces for management applications to interact with the agent, distribute or consolidate management information, and provide security. A JMX manager can control any number of agents, thereby simplifying highly distributed and complex management structures.

underlying native protocol stack and provides a "factory" to create and manage *Providers*. *Providers* exchange protocol messages with the native protocol layer using a proprietary mechanism. Therefore, the *Provider* components are specific to a particular implementation of a protocol layer. *Listener* components interact with the *Provider* component via *Event* objects. To exchange *Event* objects, *Listener* components must register with *Provider* components. *Listener* components should be portable across various implementations of Provider components. Applications use the JAIN API to implement a *Listener* interface. The *Provider* component maps the generic API to a specific flavor of a protocol, implemented by the native protocol stack.

Zero or more *Listeners* could register with a *Provider*, however, a *Provider* may limit the number of *Listeners* that may register at any one time. The *Events* are routed to and from the *Listener* and *Provider* based on a user address. For JAIN TCAP, this is a set of signaling point codes, sub-system number, and optionally global title. For JAIN ISUP, the user address is a set of signaling point codes and

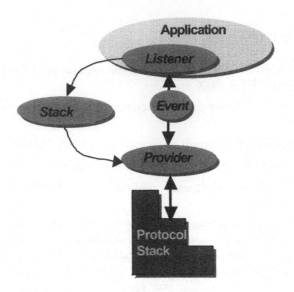

Figure 2.5 *JAIN protocol API architecture (sourced from [8]).*

circuit identification codes (CICs). For most IP protocols, SIP, MGCP, etc. there is a one for one mapping from *Listener* to *Provider,* so no user address is needed. However, in the Internet space, one could readily define a user address as a combination of ports or Internet addresses.

Each *Listener* is required to register with a unique value for this given set of parameters. Any given *Listener* may also register with multiple *Providers*. Demultiplexing of events from *Listener* to *Provider* uses a given set of parameters (e.g. protocol variant, *Provider* vendor, etc.) as defined by the corresponding JAIN SS7 API specification.

SS7 telephony

SS7 technology provides a general-purpose signaling system for use between network nodes in a telephony or wireless network. SS7 is optimized for operation in digital networks utilizing computers and is a reliable means of transferring information in correct sequence between network nodes without loss or duplication. The SS7 network implements out-of-band signaling, that is, signaling messages are exchanged over a physical connection, which is different from the link supporting voice channel. Figure 2.6 illustrates the topology of the SS7 network.

The SS7 network consists of two main physical entities:

- *Signaling point (SP)*: acts as a local exchange to the subscriber and provides an interface to the SS7 network. It also acts as a switch for voice channels and it supports database access queries for applications such as 800/freephone.

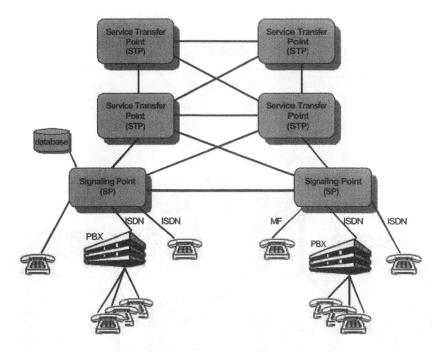

Figure 2.6   *Topology of SS7 network.*

- *Signaling transfer point (STP)*: is a router for the SS7 network. It relays messages through the network but it does not originate them.

At the core of an SS7 network, the integrated services digital network (ISDN) user part (ISUP) provides call signaling capabilities and the transaction capabilities application part (TCAP) provides remote operation invocation capabilities via transaction exchange. Applications (e.g. call control, service logic, etc.) use the services provided by ISUP and TCAP to access the signaling capabilities of the SS7 network. ISUP and TCAP use sequenced/non-sequenced, reliable/non-reliable, routing, congestion control, link management, address translation, and application de-multiplexing services provided by the three message transfer parts (MTP) and signaling connection control part (SCCP).

Intelligent networks

The call control application in basic SS7 networks has the service logic tightly coupled to the call processing logic in all switches, in the form of software. In order to provide new, improved, or upgraded services, the software in all of the switches must be upgraded. This is a very expensive and time-consuming process, considering the number of switches existing in an SS7 network. The solution to this problem is to separate out service logic from basic call processing and to concentrate the service logic in some dedicated entities in the SS7 network. Thus, when a new

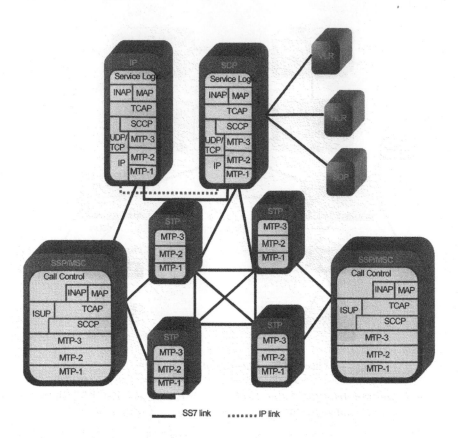

Figure 2.7 *Integrated SS7, IN and wireless network framework (sourced from [8]).*

service has to be incorporated, or existing service logic has to be upgraded, only a few entities in the telecommunication network need to be changed. In other words, the solution to the problem is to push the intelligence of the network to a few selected entities in the network. This effort enhances and reincarnates the basic SS7 network as an IN [22–35,36] (Figure 2.7).

IN architecture classifies the signaling points (SP) in an SS7 network into four different logical entities:

- *Service switching point (SSP)*: the SSP is a basic switch with enhanced capabilities for routing and detecting requests for special services. As networks converge, Softswitch technology is rapidly assuming this role in the network.

- *Service data point (SDP)*: provides subscriber data storage and access capability. This is similar to the database entity illustrated in Figure 2.6 Combined with an SCP, a service node or application server is created. The SDP contains the customer and network data, which is accessed during the execution of a service.

- *Service control point (SCP)*: provides a service logic execution environment or an application server. The SCP is fundamentally concerned about services – how they are created, deployed, destroyed, updated, provisioned, etc.

- *Intelligent peripheral (IP)*: provides resources such as customized voice announcements, voice recognition, and dual tone multi-frequencies (DTMF) digit collection. In a converged network, other intelligent peripherals may include media gateways.

SSP, SDP, SCP, and IP communicate using the IN application part (INAP) protocol layer to invoke and execute service logic. The JAIN INAP API defines the INAP interfaces from a service point of view or from the SCP/application server. INAP in the conventional SS7 definition is often layered on top of TCAP, however, the functionality and definitions within INAP have relevance to voice over IP such that INAP could potentially be run over SIP.

Network services

At the service level, there is a standard reusable network-wide set of capabilities and features used to realize services:

- *Service independent building block (SIB)*. In Java, a SIB is analogous to a JavaBean, it does not represent a complete service, but several SIBs or JavaBeans, connected together may constitute a service.

- *Service creation environments (SCE)* – a tool used to create services out of SIBs.

- *Service logic execution environment (SLEE)* – a processing environment conducive to running communications services.

The JAIN™ service logic execution environment (JSLEE) is a set of software interfaces to support and simplify the construction of portable telecommunications services (Figure 2.8). The primary goal of JSLEE is service portability: a service should be able to run unchanged on any JAIN-compliant platform. In addition to offering service portability, JSLEE simplifies service programming by providing a service framework, and by providing implementations of common service elements within this framework. Services that choose to conform to the suggested framework can take advantage of these JSLEE components, but each service provider may choose to use or not to use these components as needs dictate.

Within any network, there are various layers that handle different functionality. At the lowest layer are the protocols such as SIP, H.323, TCAP, ISUP, or special hardware entities such as trunk interfaces or circuit switching hardware. The next layer up includes a generic call control abstraction, which is known as JCC and JCAT (see Chapter 3) in the JAIN architecture. JCC and JCAT deal with calls and network triggers. A call is the familiar concept of a temporary association between parties for the purpose of real-time communication. A trigger is a point in the progression of the call state where call processing is passed over to the

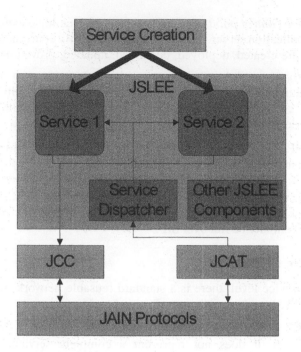

Figure 2.8 *JAIN service creation and execution environment.*

control of a *service*. It is these call-related services along with other non-call-related services that run in the JSLEE environment. In the next section, we will discuss how a *credit card calling* service is implemented using various SIBs in a SLEE.

Credit card calling (CCC)

CCC is a service which allows the user to make a call at any time, using any telephone and his/her credit card. Under this service, the call will be charged to the credit card used to make the call and not to the telephone from which the call was made. Broadly, this service involves following steps:

1. The user enters an 800 number to connect to the CCC service provider.

2. The service provider prompts the user to provide his/her personal identification number (PIN) and credit card number.

3. The user provides his PIN and credit card number.

4. The service provider authenticates the user based on the PIN provided by the user.

5. After successful authentication of the user, the service provider asks the user to provide the destination number.

6. The service provider connects the user to called party.

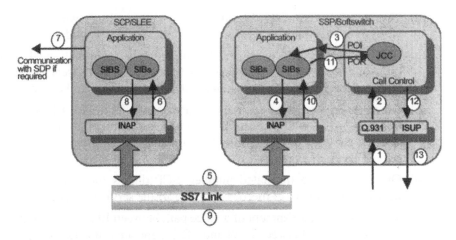

Figure 2.9 *Information flow sequence.*

Figure 2.9 illustrates a sample information flow sequence for a CCC service. Of these information flows, information flow 1 is an ISDN (Q.931) message, information flow 13 is an ISUP message, and information flows 5 and 9 are INAP messages. Now let us look at this service from an IN perspective, as illustrated by the interaction between various SIBs in Figure 2.10. From an IN perspective the following events occur at various physical entities in the network:

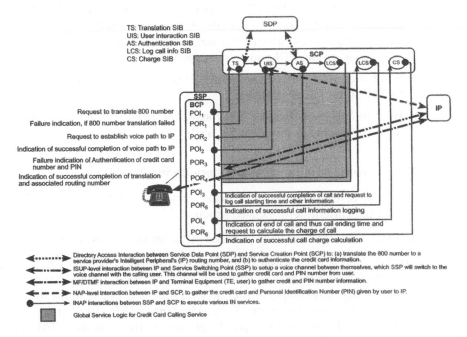

Figure 2.10 *BCP and SIB interaction to provide credit card calling service (sourced from [8]).*

(a) The user uses a terminal equipment (TE), e.g. telephone, which is connected to an SSP, to dial the 800 number of the CCC service provider.

(b) After collecting and analyzing the 800 number information, the basic call process (BCP) SIB in SSP realizes that this is an IN service. It sends an INAP message to SCP, indicating that the number has to be translated.

(c) On receiving the INAP message, SCP executes TRANSLATION SIB, which interacts with the SDP using directory access protocol to query the database and get the corresponding routing number to the service provider and other related service information.

(d) On receiving the translated number, SCP directs the SSP, using the INAP message to connect to the IP belonging to the service provider.

(e) SSP initiates establishment of a voice path between IP and itself and switches it to the voice path between itself and TE. It generates an indication to SCP, using the INAP message, on successful completion of voice path establishment.

(f) At this point SCP executes USER INTERACTION SIB, which directs the IP, using the INAP message to play an announcement, which in turn directs the user to enter his/her PIN, credit card number and destination number. The announcement between user and IP is played over the voice channel.

(g) The user enters the PIN and the destination number, which is collected by the IP and passed to SSP.

(h) On receiving the PIN, credit card number and destination number, SSP executes AUTHENTICATION SIB, which interacts with SDP to query the database storing information about the credit card. AUTHENTICATION SIB, in SSP, uses information obtained from the SDP, to authenticate the user based on the PIN and credit card number.

(i) After successful authentication of the user, SSP passes the destination number to SSP in the INAP message.

(j) BCP in SSP then resumes the connection establishment procedure using the destination number provided by SSP.

JAIN protocol APIs: a network service facilitator

Substantial investment has been made in writing software for the SS7 protocol layers in the current network infrastructure.

The JAIN SS7 API defines Java-based APIs for the following protocols:

- *TCAP [5]*: a transaction-based control protocol that provides support for message exchange between interactive applications in a distributed environment. A logical example of transaction processing in every day life is the interaction between an Automated Teller Machine (ATM) and a person, as illustrated in Figure 2.11. In this example the person interfaces to the ATM machine and has no idea how the ATM is talking to the bank. The ATM presents a single

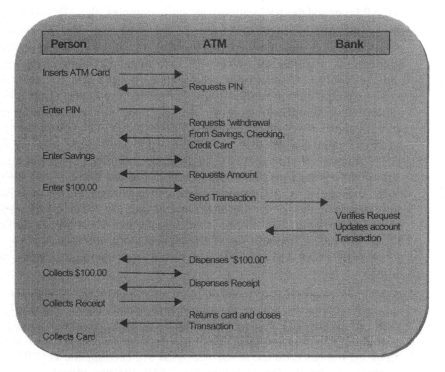

Figure 2.11 *Sample Automated Teller Machine transaction.*

interface to what are multiple interfaces. An SS7 TCAP protocol stack operates the same way. TCAP provides one interface to the application, when in reality, there may be numerous underlying interactions taking place. All the details of the transaction are not sent to the far node until the final piece of information has been gathered and checked. In the ATM example, the transaction is not completed until the person has collected the card and walked away. This is analogous to a structured dialogue in TCAP, which is not deleted until the dialogue is complete. The ATM machine handles all the error processing; similarly TCAP has to handle all possible error conditions. In the ATM example, the person could enter wrong values, enter different accounts to draw from, different amounts of money, etc. or the bank had the option to reject the request based on any of the data provided. This simple ATM example does not take into account all the complexities of money transactions, but the basic idea is to interact with a bank to exchange information, and hopefully get money. In the same way, there are many complexities needed to support SS7 TCAP processing, but the goals are the same, interact with a foreign entity to which you send and retrieve information, and hopefully get results. Although the interactions between the banking system and the ATM are quite complex, the interface to the human is quite simple. Similarly, this specification and the resultant API specification only deal with the simple interface to the functions of TCAP. While the

TCAP layer and the SS7 network are quite complex, the API specification hides the complexities so applications can focus on services. The TCAP API is only concerned with the application interface, not the SS7 implementation. The applications at signaling points (SP) exchange messages using *transactions* and *components*. Transactions represent a dialogue (or a series of message exchanges) between the applications. Components represent a specific operation requested by an application or the result of an operation requested by an application (in the context of a dialogue). The JAIN TCAP API specifies the Java interfaces and classes that are required for initializing and terminating a TCAP transaction, managing TCAP dialogue identifiers, and building and sending TCAP transactions and components. Using the JAIN TCAP API, applications, the native TCAP protocol stack can exchange TCAP transactions and components in the form of Java *Event Objects*. The JAIN TCAP API is based on the ITU'93 [3], ITU'97 [4], ANSI'92 [1], and ANSI'96 [2] variants of the TCAP protocol. Currently (as of November 2000), the final release of version 2.0 of JAIN TCAP API is available at the universal resource locator (URL) listed in [5].

- *ISUP [19]*: a call-related signaling protocol that provides support for call establishment and release and trunk circuit management in an SS7 network. Using the JAIN ISUP API, call control applications can exchange ISUP control messages with native ISUP protocol stacks in the form of Java *Event objects*. The JAIN ISUP API is based on the ANSI'92, ANSI'96, ITU'93, and ITU'97 ISUP specifications. Currently (as of November 2000), the participant review release of version 1.0 of JAIN ISUP API is available at the URL listed in [19]. Therefore, the ISUP Edit group is still working on completing this specification.

- *MAP [18]*: a non-call-related signaling protocol that provides the support for interactive mobile applications in a distributed network environment. It defines the end-to-end protocols between MAP users located in an SS7 network and another network supporting the MAP protocol. JAIN MAP API is based on the ETSI MAP GSM and IS41 TIA/EIA specifications. Using the JAIN MAP API, mobile applications can establish and release basic dialogue and perform remote operation invocation between two network entities. Currently (as of November 2000), the participant review release of version 1.0 of JAIN MAP API is available at the URL listed in [18]. Therefore, the MAP Edit group is still working on completing this specification.

- *INAP [17]*: a non-call-related signaling protocol that allows applications to communicate between various nodes/functional entities of an IN. The protocol defines the operations to be performed between SPs for providing IN services, such as number translation, time of day, follow me, etc. JAIN INAP API is based on the ANSI/Bellcore advanced intelligent network (AIN 0.2) and ITU-T CS-2 INAP specifications. Currently (as of November 2000), the participant review release of version 1.0 of JAIN INAP API is available at the URL listed in [17]. Therefore, the INAP Edit group is still working on completing this specification.

- *OAM* [20]: standard mechanisms used to provision and maintain various protocol entities in the SS7 network. OAM includes the configuration of options for hardware, routing, transmission rates and circuits. While other JAIN SS7 APIs define a generic interface in order to *exchange* protocol messages between applications and native implementations of protocol stacks, the JAIN OAM API defines a generic interface to *manage* various components in the native implementations of protocol stacks. JAIN OAM API defines a managed object (MO) for each manageable component in the SS7 network. MOs could be created and managed using tools such as Java dynamic management kit (JDMK), which is based on JMX. Using the JAIN OAM API, network management entities can easily provision and monitor various components in native implementations of protocol stacks. Currently (as of November 2000), the final release of version 2.0 of JAIN OAM API is available at the URL listed in [20].

JAIN TCAP API

This section briefly explains working of JAIN TCAP API based on the final release of version 2.0 located at the URL listed in [5]. The JAIN TCAP API is defined as a Java package, jain.protocol.ss7.tcap. Within this package, the JAIN TCAP API specification describes the following main Java components:

- *jain.protocol.ss7.tcap.JainTcapStack*: a Java interface, to be implemented by TCAP protocol stack vendors, to represent their implementation of the TCAP stack for provisioning and management.

- *jain.protocol.ss7.tcap.JainTcapProvider*: a Java interface, to be implemented by TCAP protocol stack vendors, to interact with their implementation of the TCAP stack.

- *jain.protocol.ss7.tcap.JainTcapListener*: a Java interface, to be implemented by TCAP application vendors (typically for IN and wireless services), to access TCAP services via any implementation of a *JainTcapProvider* interface.

- jain.protocol.ss7.tcap.Component: a Java package, with a standardized set of classes and associated methods, to build and process various TCAP components.

- jain.protocol.ss7.tcap.Dialogue: a Java package, with a standardized set of classes and associated methods, to build and process various TCAP transactions.

A "factory" design pattern is one in which a specific class is defined to create object instances of other classes, whose implementation is hidden. As a part of the JAIN SS7 API, a factory class, **jain.protocol.ss7.JainSS7Factory,** is defined and used to create an object instance of the class implementing *JainTcapStack*. Protocol stack vendors will provide a class **com.<CompanyName>.jain.protocol.ss7.tcap. JainTcapStackImpl,** which implements the *JainTcapStack* interface, and a class **com.<companyName>.jain.protocol.ss7.tcap.JainTcapProviderImpl,** which im-plements the *JainTcapProvider* interface.

```
/* Example #1: A JAIN TCAP example (used to send TCAP messages)
 * based on the example in JAIN TCAP API Release 2.0 available at
 * http://java.sun.com/aboutJava/communityprocess/final/jsr011/index.html
 */

/* Any TCAP User application interested in receiving dialogue
 * and component Events must implement the JainTcapListener interface.
 */
public class JainTcapListenerImpl implements JainTcapListener
{
 /* Constructor method to initialize all global variables, create
  * a provider and send a Component and Dialogue event.
  */
 public JainTcapListenerImpl ()
 {
  /* Do any necessary attribute initializations for the object of this class */
 } /* end of JainTcapListenerImpl constructor */

 /* Sample method to send an INVOKE component within BEGIN Dialogue */
 public sendTestInvoke()
 {
  /* Use the JainSS7Factory to set the desired PathName and obtain a
   * reference to a JainTcapStack object and set its Signalling Point Code
   */
  /* Obtain an instance of the Factory and set the path */
  JainSS7Factory ss7Factory = JainSS7Factory.getInstance();
  ss7Factory.setPath("com.companyName");
  JainTcapStack myTcapStack = null;
  try
  {
   myTcapStack = (JainTcapStack)
   ss7Factory.createSS7Object("jain.protocol.ss7.tcap.JainTcapStack");
   myTcapStack.setName("ANSI-92-COMPANYNAME-255-255-255");
  }
  catch (SS7PeerUnavailableException e)
  {
   /* com.companyName.jain.protocol.ss7.tcap.JainTcapStack class not found. */
   System.err.println("The specified class could not be found in
                       the CLASSPATH");
  }

  /* Use JainTcapStack Object to obtain a new JainTcapProvider */
  JainTcapProvider myTcapProvider = myTcapStack.createDetachedProvider();

  /* Note: myTcapProvider is not attached (bound) to the underlying
   *       stack so that we can now perform some initialization
   *       operation before explicitly attaching to the stack.
   */
  myTcapStack.attach(myTcapProvider);

  /* JainTcapProvider class will be used to send TCAP Component and
   * Dialogue handling primitives into the SS7 protocol stack, and
   * will be used to listen for TCAP messages from the SS7 protocol
   * stack. The User Application should register as a listener of the
   * JainTcapProvider with a User Address. Once a TCAP message
   * arrives, the Provider should inspect the Destination User Address
   * of the message and send the message as Component and Dialogue
   * handling Events to the JainTcapListener registered with the
   * Provider with that User Address.
   */

  /* Set the user address for this User Application */
  TcapUserAddress sourceUserAddr = new TcapUserAddress(Byte("0x87654321"), 0x90);


  /* Continued in the inset box on the next page................. */
```

```
/* ............... Continued from the inset box on the previous page */

/* Register this User Application as an event Listener of the Provider */
try
{
 myTcapProvider.addJainTcapListener(this, sourceUserAddr);
}
catch(TooManyListenersException e)
{
 /* Maximum number of Listeners allowed per provider have already been registered */
};

/* To send TCAP messages, we have to create Request Component Events and send
 * it to the Provider, interspersed with dialogue request Events. First a
 * request component is created as an Event, setting the Listener (this) as
 * the Event source. Parameters of the component primitive may be set using
 * the appropriate 'set' method.
 */
/* Get a new Dialogue Id for use in this Dialogue */
int dialogueId = myTcapProvider.getDialogueId();

/* Get a new Invoke Id for use within the Dialogue */
int invokeId = myTcapProvider.getInvokeId(dialogueId);

/* Create a new operation and set its parameters */
Operation op = new Operation();
op.setOperationType(Operation.OPERATIONTYPE_LOCAL);
op.setOperationFamily(Operation.OPERATIONFAMILY_REPORTEVENT);
op.setOperationSpecifier(Operation.OPERATIONSPECIFIER_REPORTEVENT);

/* Create a new InvokeReqEvent component to invoke the operation.
 * Also, set the parameters of Invoke Request event.
 */
InvokeReqEvent invokeReq = new InvokeReqEvent(this, dialogueId,
                                                    op);
invokeReq.setInvokeId(invokeId);
invokeReq.setTimeout(5000);
invokeReq.setLastInvoke(true); /* this is the last Invoke */

/* Send component request primitive to the Provider */
try
{
 myTcapProvider.sendComponentReqEvent(invokeReq);
}
catch (MandatoryParametersNotSetException e)
{
 System.err.println("Some of the required parameters were not set");
};

try
{
 /* Create a Dialogue request Event in the same way and send it to
  * the Provider after setting its parameter.
  */
 BeginReqEvent beginReq = new BeginReqEvent(this,
                                dialogueId, sourceUserAddr,
                                new TcapUserAddress(Byte("0x12345678"), 0x90));
 BeginReqEvent beginReq = new BeginReqEvent(this);
 DialoguePortion dialoguePortion = new DialoguePortion();
 dialoguePortion.setProtocolVersion(DialogueConstants.PROTOCOL_VERSION_ANSI_92);
 dialoguePortion.setAppContextName(Byte("0x12345678"));
 beginReq.setAllowedPermission(true);
 myTcapProvider.sendDialogueReqEvent((DialogueReqEvent) beginReq);

/* Continued in the inset box on the next page............... */
```

```
/* _____ Continued from the inset box on the previous page */

  /* Clean up the resources allocated */
  myTcapProvider.releaseInvokeId(invokeId);
  myTcapProvider.releaseDialogueId(dialogueId);
  }
 catch (MandatoryParametersNotSetException e)
 {
  System.err.println("Some of the required parameters were not set");
 }
} /* End of sendTestInvoke() method */

/* Method to process ComponentIndEvent */
 public void processComponentIndEvent(ComponentIndEvent event)
 {
 JainTcapProvider eventSource = event.getSource();
 /* At this stage we only know that the event is a ComponentIndEvent.
  * Therfore we need to find out the primitive type.
  */
 switch (event.getPrimitiveType())
 {
  case TcapConstants.PRIMITIVE_INVOKE:
  {
   /* Typecast to an Invoke Indication Event */
   InvokeIndEvent invokeInd = (InvokeIndEvent)event;

   /* Print the Invoke primitive */
   System.out.println(invokeInd.toString());
   return;
  } /* End of case TcapConstants.PRIMITIVE_INVOKE */

  case TcapConstants.PRIMITIVE_ERROR : {......};
  case TcapConstants.PRIMITIVE_REJECT : {......};
  case TcapConstants.PRIMITIVE_RESULT : {......};
  case TcapConstants.PRIMITIVE_LOCAL_CANCEL : {......};
  case TcapConstants.PRIMITIVE_USER_CANCEL : {......};
  default : /* not a recognised component */
 }
} /* end of processComponentIndEvent() method */

/* Processing of DialogueIndEvent */
public void processDialogueIndEvent(DialogueIndEvent event)
{
 /* Processing a Dialogue Indication Event is similar to the
  * processing of Component Indication Event.
  */
 switch (event.getPrimitiveType())
 {
  case TcapConstants.PRIMITIVE_BEGIN:
  {
   /* Typecast to a Begin Indication Event */
   BeginIndEvent beginInd = (BeginIndEvent)event;

   /* Print the Invoke primitive */
   System.out.println(beginInd.toString());
   return;
  } /* End of case TcapConstants.PRIMITIVE_BEGIN */

  case TcapConstants.PRIMITIVE_CONTINUE : {......};
  case TcapConstants.PRIMITIVE_END : {......};
  case TcapConstants.PRIMITIVE_NOTICE : {......};
  case TcapConstants.PRIMITIVE_UNIDIRECTIONAL : {......};

 /* Continued in the inset box on the next page_____. */
```

```
  /* .................Continued from the inset box on the previous page */


   case TcapConstants.PRIMITIVE_USER_ABORT : {......};
   case TcapConstants.PRIMITIVE_PROVIDER_ABORT : {......};
   default : /* not a recognised component */
  }
 }

 /* Method to Add a TcapUserAddress to the list of User Addresses
  * used by this JainTcapListener.
  */
 public void addUserAddress(TcapUserAddress userAddress)
 {
   userAddressList.addElement(userAddress);
 }

 /* Method to remove a TcapUserAddress from the list of User
  * Addresses used by this JainTcapListener.
  */
 public void removeUserAddress(TcapUserAddress userAddress)
 {
   userAddressList.removeElement(userAddress);
 }

 /* Returns the list of User Addresses used by this JainTcapListener */
 public Vector getUserAddressList()
 {
  return(this.userAddressList);
 }

 /* Initialise all variables for Listener class */
} /* end of JainTcapListenerImpl class */
```

The following is a sequence of events that occurs after the TCAP application (e.g. call control) is instantiated and before the first component is sent to the native TCAP stack:

1. Using the `JainSS7Factory.getInstance()` static method, the TCAP application creates an object instance of **JainSS7Factory** class.

2. Using the `JainSS7Factory.setPathName()` method, the TCAP application sets the path where JAIN TCAP API classes are defined as **com.<CompanyName>**.

3. Using the `JainSS7Factory.createSS7Object()` method, the TCAP application creates an object instance of class implementing the *com.<CompanyName>.jain.protocol.ss7.tcap.JainTcapStack* interface.

4. Using the `JainTcapStack.createAttachedProvider()` method, the TCAP application creates an object instance of class implementing the *com.<CompanyName>.jain.protocol.ss7.tcap.JainTcapProvider* interface. During the creation of this object, it attaches itself to the native protocol stack.

5. Using the `JainTcapProvider.addJainTcapListener()` method, the TCAP application registers with the **JainTcapProvider** class.

6. Using the `JainTcapProvider.getDialogueId()` method, the TCAP application obtains a new dialogue ID to initiate a new dialogue.

7. Using the constructors of appropriate subclass of **ComponentReqEvent**, the TCAP application creates an object instance of a TCAP Component and populates its attributes. It then sends this component towards the native TCAP stack using the `JainTcapProvider.sendComponentReqEvent()` method.

8. Using the constructors of the appropriate subclass of the **DialogueReqEvent**, the TCAP application creates an object instance of a TCAP dialogue and populates its attributes. It then sends this dialogue towards the native TCAP stack using the `JainTcapProvider.sendDialogueReqEvent()` method. This completes the initiation and the transmission of a dialogue.

A sample program to send a TCAP component and dialogue is illustrated in Example 1. Please note that this example does not provide a complete program and is therefore not executable. To execute this program, the JAIN TCAP API package, a proprietary implementation of the native TCAP protocol stack, and additional methods in the classes illustrated in the examples are needed. The purpose of this example is to demonstrate the usage of some of the important packages and classes to build and receive TCAP components and dialogues. This example is based on the examples in [5]. An application similar to Example 1 may exist in SSP/SCP/IP.

2.3.2 JAIN IP APIs

The ease with which data travels over the Internet at low cost has inspired industry pioneers to carry traditional voice and multimedia traffic over the Internet. To provide services over an IP network equivalent to those of a traditional telephone network, various new protocols, such as H.323, MGCP (media gateway control protocol), SIP (session initiation protocol) [9], and various new network entities, such as media gateways, gatekeepers, call agents and media gateway controllers, have been defined. The operation of these entities is depicted in Figure 2.12.

Figure 2.12 depicts various types of multimedia communications over an IP network, using different protocols. In a real deployment scenario, only a subset of these protocols and devices will be used:

- *Multimedia terminal*: the multimedia terminal is directly connected to the IP network and contains an implementation of the multimedia control and media protocols. The terminal could be a PC with special software, or can be a dedicated appliance, such as an IP phone. An H.323 terminal will contain an implementation of the H.323 control protocol for setting up multimedia calls. Alternative protocols for setting up multimedia calls are SIP and MGCP. In all cases, real time transport protocol (RTP) and real time transport control protocol (RTCP) are used for managing media flows.

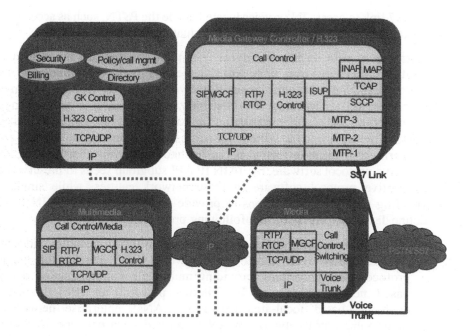

Figure 2.12 *IP network supporting multimedia traffic (sourced from [8]).*

- *Media gateway (MG)*: in order to connect the IP telephony network with the existing PSTN, there is a need for a gateway between the two networks. A media gateway connects the PSTN voice trunks to the IP network. It is a relatively simple device that translates circuit-switch voice to packet voice. In addition to terminating voice-circuit, it contains RTP/RTCP for sending packet data into the IP network and MGCP to communicate with an intelligent controller in the IP network.

- *Media gateway controller (MGC)/call agent (CA):* the MGC is complementary to the MG. It provides the control connectivity to the PSTN via an SS7 link, terminating SS7 ISUP call signaling. It controls the MG through MGCP to set up connections between the PSTN and the IP network. Furthermore, it communicates with other call signaling elements in the IP network using protocols such as H.323 and SIP. This element represents the call signaling intelligence in the IP network. In order to move this intelligence away from the edge of the IP network, it is possible to split this gateway into a signaling gateway that terminates SS7 signaling and then transports it to an intelligent controller, call agent (CA) located inside the IP network, using a protocol such as stream control transport protocol (SCTP).

- *Gatekeeper (GK)*: the gatekeeper is an H.323 control entity that controls access to resources, implements policies and provides access to other "back-end" services, such as directory lookups for call routing. It may be implemented as a standalone entity or combined with the MGC. In the latter case, it could use the

SS7 link to access IN services located inside the PSTN, such as access to number translation databases, subscriber information databases, etc.

There are a wide variety of devices and platforms that can be used to provide multimedia services over IP networks, depending on the combination of functions that are deployed in a single device. However, the services that are required by end users are well known, e.g. for telephony, services such as call waiting, caller identification, 800-number translation and calling cards are required. It is desirable to allow the services to be written in Java so that they can migrate across a variety of platforms as IP telephony networks and technologies evolve. By defining Java APIs to native protocol software, the JAIN IP API subgroup seeks to preserve the existing native protocol software in these network entities, while simultaneously enabling new Java applications to provide new services. The JAIN IP API will define Java-based APIs for the following protocols:

- *H.323*: provides support for the transmission of real-time audio, video, and data communications over packet-based networks. H.323 specifies the components, protocols, and procedures providing multimedia communication over packet-based networks, such as IP (Internet protocol) or IPX (Internet packet exchange)-based local-area networks (LANs), enterprise networks (ENs), metropolitan-area networks (MANs), and wide-area networks (WANs). H.323 defines call-set-up, the exchange of compressed audio and/or video, conferences, and interoperability with non-H.323 end points. The JAIN H.323 API is a standard, generic Java-based interface to native H.323 protocol stacks. The JAIN H.323 API facilitates the exchange of various H.323 control messages, such as H.225 call signaling, H.245 control signaling, and H.225 registration and administration, and status (RAS) services. As of November 2000, the JAIN Protocol Expert Group has yet to start working on JAIN H.323 API.

- *MGCP* [21]: defines the messages to be exchanged between CA and MG. CA, in turn, uses these messages (1) to instruct the MG to watch for specific events such as hook actions or DTMF tones on a specified endpoint, (2) to create and release connections, (3) to modify connections, and (4) to audit connections. MGs use these messages to notify CAs whenever a call is received. The JAIN MGCP API is a standard, generic Java-based interface that sends and receives MGCP control messages to and from the underlying native protocol stacks in MG and to and from call control applications in CA. The JAIN MGCP API is based on the MGCP Internet drafts and the Cable Labs PacketCable™ network-based call signaling protocol specification. Currently (as of November 2000), the public review draft of version 1.0 of JAIN MGCP API is available at the URL listed in [21].

- *SIP [15]* is an application-layer control (signaling) protocol for creating, modifying and terminating sessions with one or more participants. These sessions include Internet multimedia conferences, Internet telephone calls and multimedia distribution. Members in a session can communicate via multicast or via a mesh of unicast relations, or a combination of these. SIP is an ASCII text-based, transport-independent protocol based on a client–server model, where SIP clients issue requests and the SIP server responds to the request.

A SIP-based network

A SIP-based network (as illustrated in Figure 2.13) has the following fundamental elements:

- *Softswitches (SS) or MGCs* are devices that control the different types of MGs. A MG performs translation from one form of media into packet-based data, that is, IP packets. Media may be in the form of voice trunks, ATN, residential usage, business and virtual private networks, etc.

- *User agents* take on many forms such as IP phone, software IP phone that runs on a PC client, hand-held IP phone devices, or smart SIP endpoints with graphics displays.

- Different types of *SIP servers* include user agent, proxy, redirect, location directory, and registrar.

The purpose of SIP is to create, maintain, and eventually terminate sessions. A session is any connection that requires a point-to-point media stream – voice, data, video, etc. Figure 2.14 illustrates an example of a session set-up and teardown. The SIP client or user agent (UA) is an application program that sends SIP requests. The SIP server is an application program that accepts SIP requests. In order to service requests the SIP server sends back SIP responses for those requests. SIP is a peer-to-peer protocol, as opposed to a master–slave protocol. A SIP client could be a server

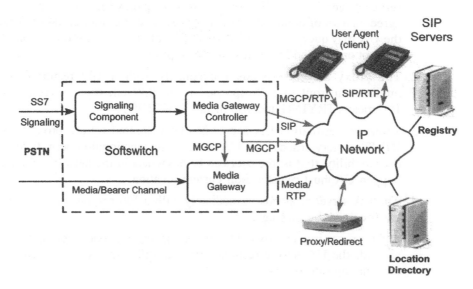

Figure 2.13 *A SIP-based network.*

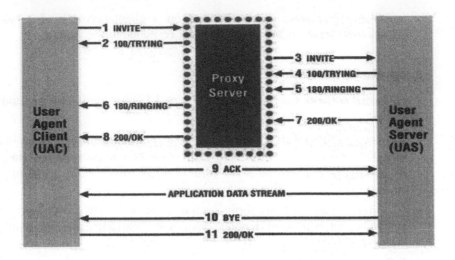

Figure 2.14 *SIP control message exchanges.*

in another transaction. SIP allows a client to send messages to any SIP-enabled server without being aware of the type of server that it is communicating with. The behavior of the SIP client is based on the responses without considering where the responses came from. Various steps involved in the example illustrated in Figure 2.14 are explained below:

1. The UA client initiates a call with the UA server, via the proxy server by sending an INVITE message to the proxy server that is destined for the UA server. Inside the INVITE is a session descriptor, which allows participants to agree on a set of compatible media types. As in the prior credit card example, the UA may query the user for the pertinent credit card information and then encrypt and imbed in the session description.

2. The proxy server responds immediately with a 100 response (different numbers in front of a "response" mean different types of responses, e.g. 100 means TRYING and 180 means RINGING).

3. After the destination UA server has been located by the proxy server, the INVITE is forwarded to the UA server. This functionality permits SIP to offer user mobility, that is, the user can be anywhere in the network. To make this happen UA must register their current location.

4. The UA server responds immediately with a 100 response to confirm that it has received the message.

5. After processing the INVITE, and notifying the end user that a call has arrived, the UA server responds with a 180 response to indicate that the terminating side is ringing.

6. The proxy server forwards the 180 responses to the UA client that originated the INVITE request.

7. After the user accepts the connection, the UA server sends a 200 response to the proxy server, indicating that the call has been accepted.

8. The proxy server forwards the 200 responses to the UA client that originated the INVITE request.

9. The UA client acknowledges that receipt of the final response to the INVITE message by sending an ACK. After the ACK, the media stream is set up and the session is in progress.

10. When either side wants to end the session, it sends a BYE request to the other side. This, as with the ACK, typically will not traverse the proxy server (unless the proxy server specifically requests this, as is the case with a firewall proxy server) since the network path is already established.

11. The UA client sends a 200 response to the UA server that originated the INVITE request.

JAIN SIP API

The JAIN SIP API is a standard, generic Java-based interface that sends and receives SIP control messages to and from the native SIP protocol stacks in SIP clients and SIP servers. The JAIN SIP API is based on the RFC 2543, published by the Internet Engineering Task Force (IETF). Currently (as of November 2000), the public review draft of version 1.0 of JAIN SIP API is available at the URL listed in [15].

The JAIN SIP API [15] is defined as a Java package, jain.protocol.ip.sip. Within this package, the JAIN SIP API specification describes the following main Java packages:

- *jain.protocol.ip.sip.JainSipStack*: a Java interface, to be implemented by SIP protocol stack vendors, to represent their implementation of the SIP stack for provisioning and management.

- *jain.protocol.ip.sip.JainSipProvider*: a Java interface, to be implemented by SIP protocol stack vendors, to interact with their implementation of the SIP stack.

- *jain.protocol.ip.sip.JainSipListener*: a Java interface, to be implemented by SIP application vendors (typically for IP telephony services), to access SIP services via any implementation of a *JainSipProvider* interface.

- jain.protocol.ip.sip.message: a Java package, with a standardized set of classes and associated methods, to build and process various SIP messages.

- jain.protocol.ip.sip.header: a Java package, with a standardized set of classes and associated methods, to build and process various SIP headers.

The following is a sequence of events that occur after the SIP application (e.g. call control) is instantiated and before the first component is sent to the native SIP stack:

1. Using the `JainIPFactory.getInstance()` static method, the SIP application creates an object instance of **JainIPFactory** class.

2. Using the `JainIPFactory.setPathName()` method, the SIP application sets the path where JAIN SIP API classes are defined to *com.<Company Name>*.

3. Using the `JainIPFactory.createIPObject()` method, the SIP application creates an object instance of class implementing the *com.<Company Name>.jain.protocol.ip.sip.JainSipStack* interface.

4. Using the `JainTcapStack.getListeningPoints()` method, on can get IP network listening points (i.e. TCP/UDP sockets) using whichever native SIP stack is receiving or sending SIP messages.

5. Using the `JainSipStack.createProvider()` method and the listening points obtained in the previous parameter as the parameter of this method, SIP application creates an object instance of class implementing the *com.<Company Name>.jain.protocol.ip.sip.JainSipProvider* interface. During the creation of this object, it attaches itself to the native protocol stack.

6. Using the `JainSipProvider.addJainSipListener()` method, the SIP application registers with the **JainSipProvider** class.

7. Using the constructors of the appropriate subclass of **RequestMessage**, the SIP application creates an object instance of a SIP Message (e.g. INVITE) and populates its attributes. It then sends this message towards the native SIP stack using the `JainSipProvider.sendRequest()` method.

A sample program to send a SIP message is illustrated in Example 2. Please note that this example does not provide a complete program and is therefore not executable. To execute this programs, JAIN SIP API package, proprietary implementation of native SIP protocol stack, and additional methods in the class illustrated in the example are required. The purpose of this example is to demonstrate usage of some of the important packages and classes to build and receive SIP messages. This example is based on the example in [15]. An application similar to Example 2 may exist in SIP phones.

2.4 SS7 and IP convergence

Due to open systems and economic forces, communications technologies are rapidly converging from multiple divergent architectures, namely the public switch telephony network (PSTN) and the Internet, into a mass cooperation between heterogeneous networks. Open systems have opened the market to numerous network suppliers, thereby driving down cost. Long distance voice transport service

```
/* Example #2: A JAIN SIP example (used to send SIP messages) based on the
 * example in JAIN SIP API Version 1.0 available at
 * http://java.sun.com/aboutJava/communityprocess/review/jsr032/index.html
 * The example looks at the code of a Jain SIP User application and the steps
 * the User application will use to create a JainSipProvider for communicating
 * with the proprietary SIP stack.
 */
/* Any SIP User application interested in receiving Message Events must implement
 * the JainSipListener interface.
 */
public class JainSipListenerImpl implements JainSipListener
{
 /* Use the JainIPFactory to set the desired PathName and obtain a reference to a
  * JainSipStack object and get its ListeningPoints.
  */
 public JainSipListenerImpl ()
 {
  /* Perform any attribute initializations for the object of this class */
 }

 /* Method to open a Session and send INVITE message */
 public sendInvite()
 {
  /* Obtain an instance of the Factory and set the path */
  JainIPFactory ipFactory = JainIPFactory.getInstance();
  ipFactory.setPath("com.companyName");
  JainSipStack mySipStack = null;
  try
  {
   mySipStack =
     (JainSipStack)ipFactory.createIPObject("jain.protocol.ip.sip.JainSipStackImpl");
   mySipStack.setName("companyName.com SIP stack");
  }
  catch (IPPeerUnavailableException e)
  {
   /* Couldn't find the class com.companyName.jain.protocol.ip.sip.JainSipStackImpl */
   System.err.println("The specified class could not be found in the CLASSPATH");
  }
  ListeningPoint[] listeningPoints = null;
  try
  {
    listeningPoints = mySipStack.getListeningPoints();
  }
  catch (ListeningPointUnavailableException e)
  {
    /* Stack has no ListeningPoints */
    System.err.println("The underlying stack currently has no ListeningPoints");
  }

  /* Use mySipStack to obtain a new JainSipProvider */
  JainSipProvider mySipProvider =
                  mySipStack.createProvider(listeningPoints[0]);

  /* Note: This Provider is attached (bound) to the underlying stack and will now
   *       receive all Message Events for the specified ListeningPoint
   */
  /* The JainSipProvider class will be used to send SIP messages into the SIP
   * stack, and will be used to listen for SIP messages from the SIP stack.
   * The User Application should register as a listener of the JainSipProviders
   * with the ListeningPoints it is interested in (each JainSipProvider has its
   * own ListeningPoint). Once a SIP message arrives, the underlying stack should
   * inspect the Request URI of the message and pass the message as a Message
   * Event to the JainSipProvider with that ListeningPoint. That JainSipProvider
   * will then send the Message Event to all its registered JainSipListeners.
   */
  /* Register this User Application as an event Listener of the Provider */
  try
  {
   mySipProvider.addJainSipListener(this);
  }

  /* Continued in the inset box on the next page............. */
```

```
/* ............ Continued from the inset box on the previous page */

catch(TooManyListenersException e)
{
 /* Maximum number of Listeners allowed per provider have already been registered */
}

/* Create Request event message and send to provider */.
/* Create a Source Address */
SipURL sourceAddress = new SipURL("Source",
                             mySipProvider.getListeningPoint().getHost());
sourceAddress.setPort(mySipProvider.getListeningPoint().getPort());
NameAddress from = new NameAddress("Source", sourceAddress);

/* Create a Destination Address */
SipURL destAddress = new SipURL("Destination",
                           mySipProvider.getListeningPoint().getHost());
destAddress.setPort(mySipProvider.getListeningPoint().getPort());
NameAddress to = new NameAddress("Destination", destAddress);

/* Create SDP body for use within InviteMessage */
............

/* create RequestURI for use within InviteMessage */
URI requestURI = (URI)destAddress.clone();
((SipURL)requestURI).setTransport(
                      mySipProvider.getListeningPoint().getTransport());

/* Send Message */
int clientTransactionId = -1;
try
{
 /* Send INVITE */
 clientTransactionId = mySipProvider.sendInvite(this, requestURI,
                                        sourceAddress, destAddress,
                                        body, "application", "sdp");

 /* Do any additional operations if required .......... */
 /* Send BYE */
 clientTransactionId = mySipProvider.sendBye(this, (InviteMessage)
             mySipProvider.getClientTransactionRequest(clientTransactionId));
}
catch(SipException e)
{
 e.printStackTrace();
}
} /* end of sendInvite() method */

/* Processing of Request Message received. */
public void processRequest(RequestMessage request, int transactionId)
{
 JainSipProvider eventSource = (JainSipProvider)request.getSource();

 /* At this stage we only know that the event is a Request Message therefore we
  * need to find out the request method.
  */
 String method = request.getMethod();

 /* Check if we received INVITE */
 if (method.equals(InviteMessage.method))
 {
  try
  {
   eventSource.sendResponse(transactionId, ResponseMessage.OK);
  }
  catch (TransactionDoesNotExistException e)
  {
   System.err.println(e.getMessage());
  }

 /* Continued in the inset box on the next page............ */
```

```
/* ............ Continued from the inset box on the previous page */

 catch (SipException e)
 {
  System.err.println(e.getMessage());
 }
}
else
{
 /* Check if we received BYE */
 if (method.equals(ByeMessage.method))
 {
  try
  {
   eventSource.sendResponse(transactionId, ResponseMessage.OK);
  }
  catch (TransactionDoesNotExistException e)
  {
   System.err.println(e.getMessage());
  }
  catch (SipException e)
  {
   System.err.println(e.getMessage());
  }
 }
 else
 {
  /* Check if we received ACK */
  if (method.equals(AckMessage.method))
  {
   processAck(((AckMessage)request), transactionId);
  }
  else
  {
   /* Check if we received CANCEL */
   if (method.equals(CancelMessage.method))
   {
    processCancel(((CancelMessage)request)), transactionId);
   }
   else
   {
    /* We received an invalid message */
    try
    {
     eventSource.sendResponse(transactionId, ResponseMessage.METHOD_NOT_ALLOWED);
    }
    catch (TransactionDoesNotExistException e)
    {
     System.err.println(e.getMessage());
    }
    catch (SipException e)
    {
     System.err.println(e.getMessage());
    }
   } /* end of invalid else */
  } /* end of CANCEL else */
 } /* end of ACK else */
} /* end of BYE else */
} /* end of processRequest() method */

/* Processing of Ack Message received */
public void processAck(AckMessage ack, int transactionId)
{
 JainSipProvider eventSource = (JainSipProvider)ack.getSource();
 System.out.println("Received AckMessage on " + eventSource.getListeningPoint());
}

/* Continued in the inset box on the next page............. */
```

```
/* ―――――― Continued from the inset box on the previous page */

/* Processing of Cancel Message received */
public void processCancel(CancelMessage cancel, int transactionId)
{
 JainSipProvider eventSource = (JainSipProvider)cancel.getSource();
 System.out.println("Received CancelMessage on " + eventSource.getListeningPoint());
}

/* Processing of Response Message received */
public void processResponse(ResponseMessage response, int transactionId)
{
 JainSipProvider eventSource = (JainSipProvider)response.getSource();
 String reasonPhrase =
         ResponseMessage.getStandardReasonPhrase(response.getStatusCode());
 System.out.println("Received ResponseMessage with a status \" + reasonPhrase + "\"");
}

/* Processing of transaction timeout.
public void processTimeout(int transactionId, boolean isServerTransaction)
{
 System.out.println("Transaction " + transactionId + " timed out");
 }
} /* end of JainSipListenerImpl class */
```

is becoming an inexpensive commodity. Carriers and service providers now have to differentiate themselves by providing enhanced services.

The challenge for telephone service provider or the Internet service provider is to attempt to present a single look and feel to what may in fact be multiple divergent networks. The consumer does not care whether his voice is carried on data or analog trunks, the consumer only cares that the provider has given a strong reliable connection with some enhanced services. While data networks reliability may be different across markets, lost data is not tolerated. Phone companies have been doing this for years. Under any given voice network one or more network architectures (e.g. PSTN or voice-over-packet (VoP)) may be supporting voice signaling and traffic. To provide truly seamless connections, it is necessary to interwork between circuit-based PSTN and the emerging voice-over-packet (VoP) networks. This interworking is achieved using elements, such as gateways and gatekeepers that straddle network boundaries and allow media information, call signaling and services to flow across the diverse networks.

JAIN technology is ideally suited to enable applications to migrate smoothly across diverse networks. As the JAIN APIs abstract the network details, the applications become network-agnostic. The following examples will illustrate the applicability of JAIN APIs in this context:

(1) One example relates to access of intelligent network services, such as 800-number translation, from voice-over-IP (VoIP) networks, as depicted in Figure 2.15. The multimedia terminal (VoIP client) initiates a call to an 800-number. Existing telephony networks have a tremendous amount of data already available in their databases, or SCPs. The VoIP call request is typically routed by a gate-

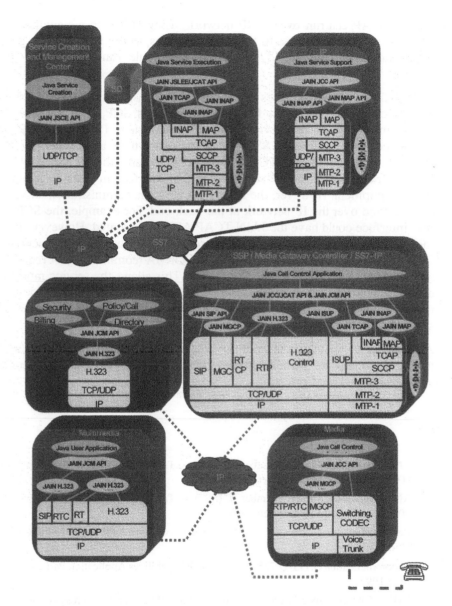

Figure 2.15 *Integrated Java-enabled multimedia network (sourced from [8]).*

keeper element in the VoIP cloud, which will then need to access data in the SCPs. Such access is typically achieved using the SS7 TCAP protocol. However, a gatekeeper application written in Java could use a JAIN TCAP API to communicate with the database. The TCAP protocol can run over traditional SS7 transport, requiring the gatekeeper to have an SS7 interface. In the picture below, this would imply that the gatekeeper and the signaling gateway are collocated. Alternately, TCAP can run over an IP network, using SCTP, to a signaling gateway, which then provides access to the database. Thus, in this scenario, the gatekeeper application can provide SS7-based services while running on top of an IP network.

(2) Another example involves the use of an IP transport network for IN services. In this case, the traditional IN elements such as SCP, SDP, service creation environment (SCE) or service management system (SMS) and IP are not connected over traditional SS7 transport, rather they are connected to an IP network. TCAP runs over TCP/IP and serves to carry the IN messages over the IP network. The SCP and IP still have an SS7 interface in order to connect to the PSTN equipment. However, the IN service creation, administration and execution can be done over the IP network at the back end. For example, the SCP with the SS7 interface could have the JAIN TCAP API implemented. However, the service logic that uses the API can execute in a remote server using an abstraction such as Java RMI (remote method invocation) or CORBA (common object request broker architecture) that runs over the IP network. This allows the service modules to be distributed across the network, instead of being inside a single device, and the modules can be upgraded dynamically without affecting the operation of other service modules.

As network technologies and protocols proliferate, the ability to write Java-based applications that are portable across various networks will become increasingly attractive and cost-effective.

References

1. ANSI Signaling System Number 7 (SS7) – Transaction Capabilities Application Part (TCAP), T1.114, ANSI, September 1992.

2. ANSI Signaling System Number 7 (SS7) – Transaction Capabilities Application Part (TCAP), T1.114, ANSI, March 1996.

3. Recommendation Q.771-Q.775 – Transaction Capabilities Application Part (TCAP), ITU-T, March 1993.

4. Recommendation Q.771-Q.775 – Transaction Capabilities Application Part (TCAP), ITU-T, June 1997.

5. JAIN TCAP API Specification, Version 2.0, Final Release, Sun Microsystems Inc., September 2000: http://java.sun.com/aboutJava/communityprocess/final/jsr011/index.html

6. JavaBeans API Specification (v1.01), Sun Microsystems Inc., July 1997: http://java.sun.com/products/javabeans/

7. De Keijzer J, Tait D, Goedman R.JAIN: a new approach to service in communication networks. IEEE Communication January 2000;94–99.

8. Bhat RR, Gupta R. JAIN protocol APIs. IEEE Communication January 2000; 100–107.

9. Handley M, Schulzrinne H, Schooler E, Rosenberg J. RFC 2543: SIP – session initiation protocol. March 1999.

10. EJB: http://java.sun.com/products/ejb

11. Jini: http://java.sun.com/products/jini

12. JavaSpaces: http://java.sun.com/products/JavaSpaces

13. Jiro: http://java.jiro.org

14. JES: http://java.sun.com/products/jtapi

15. JAIN SIP API Specification, Version 1.0, Public Review Draft, Sun Microsystems Inc., November 2000: http://java.sun.com/aboutJava/communityprocess/review/jsr032/index.html

16. Java Community Process^{SM} Program Version 1.0, Sun Microsystems Inc., December 1998: http://java.sun.com/aboutJava/communityprocess/java_community_process.html

17. JAIN INAP API Specification, Version 1.0, Participant Review, Sun Microsystems Inc., November 2000: http://java.sun.com/aboutJava/communityprocess/participant/jsr035/index.html

18. JAIN MAP API Specification, Version 1.0, Participant Review, Sun Microsystems Inc., November 2000: http://java.sun.com/aboutJava/communityprocess/participant/jsr029/index.html

19. JAIN ISUP API Specification, Version 1.0, Participant Review, Sun Microsystems Inc., September 2000: http://java.sun.com/aboutJava/communityprocess/participant/jsr017/index.html

20. JAIN OAM API Specification, Version 2.0, Final Release, Sun Microsystems Inc., September 2000: http://java.sun.com/aboutJava/communityprocess/final/jsr018/index.html

21. JAIN MGCP API Specification, Version 1.0, Public Review Draft, Sun Microsystems Inc., January 2001, http://java.sun.com/aboutJava/communityprocess/review/jsr023/index.html

22. Q.1200, General Series Intelligent Network Recommendation Structure, ITU-T.

23. Q.1201, Principles of Intelligent Network Architecture, ITU-T.

24. Q.1202, Intelligent Network – Service Plane Architecture, ITU-T.

25. Q.1203, Intelligent Network – Global Functional Plane Architecture, ITU-T.

26. Q.1204, Intelligent Network – Distributed Functional Plane Architecture, ITU-T.

27. Q.1205, Intelligent Network – Physical Plane Architecture, ITU-T.

28. Q.1208, General aspects of the Intelligent Network Application Protocol (INAP), ITU-T.

29. Q.1210, Q.1210-Series Intelligent Network Recommendation Structure, ITU-T.

30. Q.1211, Introduction to Intelligent Network Capability Set 1.

31. Q.1213, Intelligent Network – Global Functional Plane Architecture of CS-1, ITU-T.

32. Q.1214, Intelligent Network – Distributed Functional Plane Architecture of CS-1, ITU-T.

33. Q.1215, Intelligent Network – Physical Plane Architecture of CS-1, ITU-T.

34. Q.1218, Intelligent Network – Interface Recommendation for CS-1, ITU-T.

35. Q.1219, Intelligent Network User's Guide for CS-1, ITU-T.

36. Faynberg I, Gabuzda L, Lu H-L. Converged Networks and Services: Internetworking IP and the PSTN. New York: John Wiley & Sons, 2000, pp. 93–114.

3

Java call control

Ravi Jain and Farooq Anjum

Applied Research, Telcordia Technologies, USA

3.1 Introduction

Future telecommunications networks will be characterized by new and evolving architectures where packet-switched, circuit-switched, and wireless networks are integrated to offer subscribers an array of innovative multimedia, multi-party applications. Equally importantly, it is expected that the process by which telecommunications applications are developed will change, and will no longer solely be the domain of the telecommunications network or service provider. In fact, in order to provide a broad portfolio of novel, compelling applications rapidly, service providers will increasingly turn to third-party applications developers and software vendors. Thus application development in the telecommunications domain will become more similar to that in the software and information technology in general, with customers reaping the benefits of increased competition, reduced time-to-market, and rapid leveraging of new technology as it is developed.

To make this vision a reality it is necessary that future integrated networks offer application developers a set of standard, open application programming interfaces (APIs) so that applications written for one vendor's system can run on a different vendor's system. This will enable the cost of applications development to be amortized, reducing the final cost to the customer. The JAIN™ community is a community of companies led by Sun Microsystems under the Java Community

Process that is developing standard, open, published Java™ APIs for next-generation systems consisting of integrated internet protocol (IP) or asynchronous transport mode (ATM), public switched telephone network (PSTN) and wireless networks. These APIs include interfaces at the protocol level, for different protocols like MGCP[1], SIP, and TCAP, as well as at higher layers of the telecommunications software stack.[2]

One of the key APIs being developed at the higher layers of the telecommunications stack is the API for defining the *call model* that the network offers the applications developer. The call model can be regarded as a specialized virtual[3] machine for the development of telecommunications applications [1,2], with the API being the interface to that virtual machine. In this chapter we describe such an API developed by a subgroup of JAIN, called the Java call control (JCC). We stress here that the use of the phrase "call model", which has traditionally been associated with the PSTN, does not imply that the work of the JCC Edit Group is focused on the PSTN. The charter of the JCC group is to develop an API that applies equally well to IP or ATM, PSTN, and wireless networks, as well as networks integrating these technologies.

The development of open network APIs using Java represents an important departure from traditional methods by which the PSTN was made more open. In the past, advanced intelligent network (AIN) defined models that allowed the creation of services outside switches, but typically these services were written in specialized languages, using specialized service creation environments, by specialized personnel. The benefits and potential pitfalls of using Java as a language for implementing telephony APIs have been discussed in [3], and for implementing protocols in [4]. We will not repeat these discussions here; the reader is referred to [3,4]. However, we point out that aside from the benefits of the Java language itself (such as portability across different execution platforms), using Java allows the arsenal of Java-based technologies (Java Beans, Enterprise JavaBeans, etc.) to be applied to service development for telecommunications services. In addition, the growing number of tools, support utilities, development environments, and experienced programmers and designers available for Java potentially opens up large economies of scale in the service creation process. Finally, we have previously implemented a prototype call-processing platform in 100% pure Java that completes basic calls, performs advanced services, and also allows dynamic service deployment [1,2].

This chapter is organized as follows. In Section 2 we will briefly survey existing call models and APIs, including AIN, JTAPI, and Parlay. In Section 3 we describe the

---

[1]   A list of acronyms is given at the end of the book.
[2]   Many of the product and service names mentioned in this paper are trademarks or service marks of their respective owners.
[3]   Not to be confused with the Java Virtual Machine (JVM). The virtual machine we refer to here is offered to the application by the software layer implementing the API. There may be a JVM below this layer if the application is written in Java.

architecture and design of the JCC version 1.0 API and its components in some detail, focusing on a narrative explanation of its principal features rather than a line-by-line retelling of the specification. *(Note that this material is not a substitute for the specification itself, which is the definitive source. The specification is available freely from the Sun Java website, currently at http://java.sun.com/aboutJava/community-process/final.html.)* In Section 4 we illustrate the use of the JCC 1.0 API with two examples. The first example is a simple two-party call origination, while the second example illustrates the power of the JCC API in allowing standardized as well as customized event filtering during the invocation of applications. In Section 5 we present a more detailed discussion of the relationship of JCC with JTAPI and Parlay call control, focusing on how the structure of JCC is designed to allow logical compatibility with these other APIs and the industry segments that the three APIs address. Finally in Section 6 we end with some brief concluding remarks.

3.2 Call models and APIs

The JCC API defines a programming interface to next-generation converged networks in terms of an abstract, object-oriented specification. As such it is designed to hide the details of the specifics of the underlying network architecture and protocols from the application programmer to the extent possible. Thus, the network may consist of the PSTN, a packet (IP or ATM) network, a wireless network, or a combination of these, without affecting the development of services using the API. The API is also independent of network signaling and transport protocols. Thus, the network may be using various call control protocols and technologies, for example, SGCP, MGCP, SIP, H.323, ISUP, DSS1/Q.931, and DSS2/Q.2931, without the explicit knowledge of the application programmer. Indeed, different legs of a call may be using different signaling protocols and be on different underlying networks.

It is assumed that the network will be able to notify the platform implementing the API regarding events that have occurred and the platform will be able to process the event as necessary and inform the application using the API. In addition, the application will be able to initiate actions using the API that the platform will translate into appropriate protocol signaling messages to the network. It is the job of the platform to interface to the underlying network(s) and translate API methods and events to and from underlying signaling protocols as it sees fit. We stress that this translation is vendor-specific and is not specified by the API; thus different platform vendors may differentiate and compete based on the attributes (e.g. performance) of their translation.

Traditionally, the word "call" in the PSTN evokes associations with a two-party, point-to-point voice call. In contrast, in this chapter and within the JAIN JCC Edit Group, we use the word *call* to refer in general to a multimedia, multi-party, multi-protocol communications *session* over the underlying integrated (IP, ATM, PSTN, wireless) network. By "multi-protocol" we mean here that different legs of the call, representing the logical connection to individual parties of the call, may be affected by different underlying communications protocols over different types of networks. Thus, one leg of the call may be affected using the H.323 protocol [5], another via SIP [6], and a third via traditional PSTN signaling protocols like ISUP [7]. JCC can be used to set up multimedia sessions, provided they can be modeled using the abstractions provided by the JCC API. Note, however, that JCC is not intended to provide fully-fledged control of multimedia streams, such as synchronization facilities, control of different substreams, etc., these would be provided by additional packages built on top of JCC.

Several call models and associated APIs have been developed in the past, including AIN [8], Java telephony API (JTAPI) [9,3], and telephony API (TAPI) [10]. While there are important differences among these call models, reflecting the architecture or application for which they were intended, their overall goal is generally similar: to initiate, control and manipulate calls, and to facilitate the development of applications that execute before, during or after a call. Rather than select any one particular call model, we believe it is worthwhile to learn from the experience gathered by the different communities that have developed existing call models, and develop a generic call model suitable for integrated next-generation networks.

For example, the AIN call model was designed to allow applications to be developed for the PSTN. Thus, the AIN call model implicitly assumes a specific distributed architecture where telephone switches perform the basic call processing functions. It is assumed that value-added services (e.g. toll-free number translation, time-of-day call routing, etc.) are executed, before or during calls, by a specialized service logic execution environment (SLEE) like the service control point (SCP).

In contrast, JTAPI focuses on call processing and applications for a private branch exchange (PBX) or call center environment, where a much greater degree of centralized processing and control is the norm. Thus, unlike AIN, JTAPI contains no facilities for suspending execution of call processing and invoking applications during call set-up or mid-call. On the other hand, unlike AIN, JTAPI offers convenient, object-oriented abstractions for call manipulation, which facilitate the rapid development of object-oriented applications.

A survey of all existing call models we have considered is outside the scope of this chapter. In the following subsections we briefly review three existing call models and APIs that are especially relevant to our efforts, namely AIN, JTAPI and Parlay.

3.2.1 Advanced intelligent network (AIN)

In terms of the service creation process, the AIN architecture represented an important advance when it was introduced. AIN separated service development from switching, allowing service logic to be developed more quickly and placed in specialized network elements attached to databases, e.g. the service control point (SCP), while switches could be optimized for speed and efficiency.

To do this, AIN introduces a call model that consisted essentially of two major elements. The first element is a pair of finite state machines representing the progress of a call as it is processed at the originating and terminating switch, respectively. The second is the concept of *triggers*. Triggers can be defined at specific states of the originating or terminating switch's finite state machine (FSM). When call processing reaches a state in the FSM where a trigger is defined and enabled, processing is suspended and a program (called *service logic*) executing at a remote network element like the SCP is invoked; call processing is resumed once the service logic completes execution.

Note that the definition of the AIN call model can be regarded as *switch-centric*, in the sense that the fundamental activity is seen as call processing in the switch, while the service logic (which is not even dignified by being called an application program) is viewed as an ancillary activity. The application programmer must understand the details of the originating and terminating FSMs and interact with call processing at pre-specified states in the FSMs. There is no explicit abstraction offered to allow the programmer to manipulate entire calls, or legs of a call, or the principal logical entities in the call (e.g. the calling or called party's address or phone number), and certainly not in any object-oriented fashion. Enhancements built around AIN (e.g. ITU's Connection View [11]) offer facilities for modeling and manipulating calls, but these are also quite limited; for instance, at present, multi-party calls of more than three parties cannot be handled. Nonetheless, the AIN FSMs do capture the critical stages of call processing and states where it would be useful for application programs to intervene.

3.2.2 Java Telephony API (JTAPI)

JTAPI [9] is a portable, object-oriented interface for Java-based computer-telephony applications. In the following, a "call" refers to a communications session among two or more parties; each party is informally said to be participating in one "leg" of the call. Thus, a call has as many call legs (or connections) as the number of parties in the call. JTAPI is expressed in Java and defines a core call model to support basic call set-up, and a number of extensions, mostly designed to model call center features, multi-party conference calls, call routing, etc. The core model consists of a few telephony classes and their relationships, as shown in Figure 3.1. Each object in the figure corresponds to a physical or a logical entity in the telephone world. The **Provider** is an abstraction of a telephony service provider. A **Provider** class manages **Call** objects, representing calls at various stage of progress. (Note that in the description of JTAPI, as in the rest of this paper, capitalized words such as "Call" refer to specific objects in a model or API, while their lower-case counterparts such as "call" refer to the generic underlying concept such as a communication session.)

A **Provider** maintains a collection of static **Terminal** and **Address** objects in its domain. **Terminal** objects represent the physical endpoint of a call, while **Address**

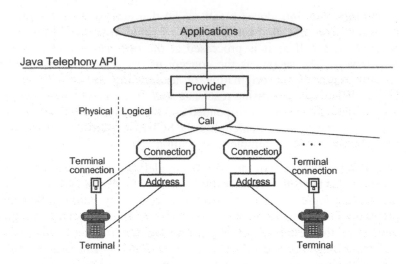

Figure 3.1   *Objects in the JTAPI model.*

objects are logical endpoints. Notice that each **Address** can be associated with multiple **Terminals** and vice versa, reflecting the standard configuration for a call center. The **Call**, **Connection**, and **Terminal Connection** objects are created dynamically, on a per-call basis. The **Call** object models the state and operations of the call as a whole, i.e. the communications session among the different parties. Each leg of the call is separately modeled by means of the **Connection** object. More precisely, the **Connection** object models the state and operations of the logical association between a **Call** and a particular **Address**. Finally, a **Terminal Connection** represents state and operations of the logical relationship between one **Connection** and one **Terminal** object.

The state of a telephone call is maintained by finite state machines associated with **Call**, **Connection** and **Terminal Connection** objects (e.g. when a call is answered by the called party, the originating **Connection** object moves to the CONNECTED state). The complete definition of the state machines is part of the published JTAPI specifications [9].

It is clear from this brief description that JTAPI overcomes several of the limitations of AIN mentioned earlier. JTAPI offers the programmer clear, explicit abstractions for manipulating calls and the logical entities in a call. The API is object-oriented, and draws upon the advantages of Java by using inheritance for extensibility. The state of a call (maintained largely in the **Connection** object FSM) is encapsulated so that it can be manipulated only via accessor methods. JTAPI uses Java exceptions and the Java events model for reporting changes in state as well as other events of interest to the application.

Nonetheless, JTAPI also has some drawbacks. The first is that the FSM in the **Connection** object is not as rich and detailed as AIN's, and even with the call control extension package cannot represent all the states of call processing that AIN does. Thus, not all the points in the call that may be of interest to applications are modeled. The second is that JTAPI does not contain any mechanism similar to AIN triggers, i.e. no mechanism to suspend call processing at a defined state in the FSM, invoke an application, and returns results.

Finally, JTAPI seems to be oriented towards providing support for developing applications in two types of scenario: (1) where applications run on a single platform (e.g. a PBX); and (2) where applications run on a platform that is "horizontally partitioned", i.e. the higher layers of software (the application and the JTAPI layer) communicate via Java remote method invocation (RMI) [12] with the lower layers over a network. Also, in JTAPI a **Provider** is assumed to be in control of all the legs of a call (they all hang off the same **Call** object managed by the **Provider**). While this assumption may add to the convenience of managing a centralized call center, it is not realistic in the broader setting of integrated next-generation networks.

As we will describe in later sections, the JCC API is attempting to build upon the best aspects of JTAPI and AIN while avoiding their drawbacks. This is possible because JCC deployment is not necessarily switch-bound. It is thus possible to extend JTAPI-style call control beyond the traditional call center boundaries, while supporting AIN-style third-party service invocation.

3.2.3 Parlay

Parlay is a multi-vendor forum founded in 1998 to specify open APIs. Initially membership was closed, with five member companies in Phase 1 and 11 in Phase 2, but with Parlay 3.0 it has been opened. The Parlay 3.0 specification for call control is expected in mid-2001.

The Parlay API describes two sets of interfaces: framework interfaces, which provide for the common functions that are required to enable services to work together in a coherent fashion, and service interfaces, which provide for the common functions that deliver whole complex services or sub-components of services (micro-services.) The Service Interfaces include the Parlay call control API. In Phase 1 of the API, the overall areas of focus were authentication, event notification, integrity management, OA&M, and service discovery. Phase 2 of the Parlay APIs expanded the scope to include IP network control, mobility, performance management, audit capabilities, and improved integrity. The plan for the next phase of Parlay includes generic charging/billing, policy management, and virtual home environment (VHE).

Clearly, the scope of Parlay is much larger than simply call control, but the Parlay call control API has received a great deal of attention. Each iteration of the Parlay call control API has undergone significant changes, and backward compatibility has not always been maintained. The design of JCC 1.0 was driven by a desire to minimize the incompatibilities between the Parlay call control API and the JCC API. We will discuss the relationship between Parlay, JTAPI and JCC APIs later in this chapter.

3.2.4 Java call control

The JCC Edit Group has developed an API that provides an interface to a generic call model that captures the essential aspects of existing call models. The API thus provides the applications programmer with a convenient and powerful abstraction for manipulating calls and managing the interaction between the application and calls. In addition, the API is extensible, so that as additional functions are required, they can be added incrementally and in a modular fashion to the API. To understand JCC it is helpful to understand the scope and context within which it is being defined.

The JAIN standardization effort is organized in two broad areas: a Protocols Expert Group (PEG) standardizing interfaces to PSTN and IP signaling protocols and an Application Expert Group (AEG) dealing broadly with the APIs required for service creation within a Java framework. Each expert group is organized as a collection of edit groups dealing with specific protocols or APIs.

Telcordia has been active in several aspects of the JAIN effort, including providing critical input to the JAIN TCAP Edit Group within the PEG which is standardizing a Java interface to TCAP, as well as being the edit lead company for the MGCP specification. Telcordia has also taken a lead position within the AEG; in particular, Telcordia is the edit group lead for the JAIN Edit Group standardizing interfaces for JCC. Other member companies of the JCC Edit Group for JCC 1.0 are AePONA, British Telecom, IBM, Lucent Technologies, Motorola, Nortel Networks, Sun Microsystems and Ulticom. In addition, in order to align JCC with JTAPI and Parlay, Telcordia interacted extensively with member companies of these groups, in particular Ericsson and Siemens.

The JCC application programming interface (API) is a Java interface for creating, monitoring, controlling, manipulating and tearing down communications sessions in a converged PSTN, packet-switched, and wireless environment. It provides facilities for first-party as well as third-party applications, and is applicable to network elements (such as switches or call agents) both at the network periphery (e.g. Class 5 or end-office switches) and at the core (e.g. Class 4 or tandem switches).

JCC allows applications to be invoked or triggered during session set-up in a manner similar in spirit to the way in which IN or AIN services can be invoked. JCC thus allows programmers to develop applications that can execute on any platform that supports the API, increasing the market for their applications. It also allows service providers to rapidly and efficiently offer services to end users by developing the services themselves, by outsourcing development, purchasing services developed by third parties, or a combination thereof.

The API is not intended to open up telecommunications networks' signaling infrastructure for public usage. Rather, network capabilities are intended to be encapsulated and made visible using object technology in a secure, manageable, and billable manner. This approach allows independent service developers to develop applications supported by the network without compromising network security and reliability.

The API is specified in terms of a coherent collection of related and interacting objects that model different physical and logical elements involved in a session, and related functions. Applications interact with these objects via an object-oriented Listener paradigm. Note that the API is applicable to control of voice, data or multimedia sessions, and not just voice calls, but for convenience we often use the word "call" in the specification.

The API is structured into the following three functional areas; this document describes only the first two (Figure 3.2).

- **Elementary call control: JCP.** The *Java call processing (JCP)* package includes the very basic facilities required for monitoring calls. It is likely that the facilities offered by this package will be too elementary for many if not most carrier-grade deployments. However, as explained later, it represents an important conceptual cornerstone for unifying the call control APIs developed by the Java Telephony API (JTAPI), JAIN and Parlay expert groups. It also represents a simple first step of software that can then be implemented, tested, reused and logically extended to a full implementation of the JCC API.

- **Core call control: JCC.** The *JCC* package includes the facilities required for observing, initiating, answering, processing and manipulating calls, as well as invoking applications and returning results during call processing. It is likely that the facilities offered by this package will suffice for implementing most, but not all, of the basic and value-added services offered by carriers.

- **Extended call control: JCAT.** The *Java coordination and transactions (JCAT)* package includes facilities similar to JCC, but extended to provide finer granu-

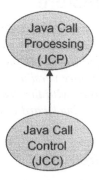

Figure 3.2 *JCP and JCC inheritance relationship.*

larity of call control. In particular, unlike JCC, JCAT enables all common AIN applications as well as other integrated voice/data and next-generation services.

For all the packages above, applications may be executing on the switching platform itself (e.g. a softswitch or Call Agent platform) or in a coordinated, distributed fashion across multiple general-purpose or special-purpose platforms.

The JCC and JCP APIs define four objects, which model the key call processing objects manipulated by most services. These are a **Provider**, **Call**, **Connection**, and **Address**. Several of these objects contain finite state machines that model the state of a call, and provide facilities for allowing applications to register and be invoked, on a per-user basis, when relevant points in call processing are reached.

The JCP and JCC APIs described in this document are intended to be consistent with the APIs issued by the JTAPI and Parlay groups. In the case of JTAPI, the JCP API represents an elementary call control package that forms the common base of both JCC and JTAPI; thus JCC and JTAPI are very consistent in this respect. In the case of Parlay, JCC is supposed to be the Java version of the Parlay API for call control as accepted by the JAIN Service Provider API (SPA) group that is standardizing Java instantiations of the Parlay API. However, as of writing, the Java version of the Parlay call control API (i.e. JCC) is similar but, unfortunately, not functionally identical to the UML version of the Multi-party Call Control Service package of the Parlay call control API; it is hoped that future revisions to the JCC and Parlay call control APIs will close this gap.

We would like to remark here that the JACC API deliberately does not address the issue of how the API would be implemented in a distributed environment with multiple providers. This is left as something to be worked out by individual implementations. We do believe, however, that a distibuted implementation of JCC is possible. In particular, our group has previously implemented a distributed version of enhanced JTAPI in the CitiTime [1] project and our experience shows that a similar implementation of JCC should be possible also.

3.3 Java call control architecture

In this section we describe the design and structure of JCC 1.0. *Note that this is intended as a general description only to provide an aid to understanding the specification, and is not a substitute for the specification itself, which is the definitive source. Also note that future versions of JCC may not necessarily be identical or compatible with JCC 1.0 or with the description given here, although of course efforts will be made to retain backward compatibility.*

3.3.1 Service drivers and requirements

The design of JCC is driven by a set of service drivers, which are specified explicitly in each release of the specification document. In addition to supporting two-party and multi-party calls, for the first release, it is required that the API support:

- *Virtual private network (VPN):* this is a corporate service that provides companies with a way to link different sites with a uniform and private dialing plan, regardless of geographical boundaries. The main function of a VPN application is to translate dialed (VPN) numbers into a routable directory number (e.g. phone number). Thus, a user need only dial, say "1 1212" and the application will translate this into the phone number of a remote site (say, "1 973 829 1212").

- *Click-to-dial (CTD):* CTD is a hybrid Internet/PSTN service that allows a terminal user browsing WWW pages to request a call set-up by simply clicking a number or name displayed on the terminal. This service is particularly useful for providing catalogue shopping, banking or travel agent online services with the capability of letting a user speak to an agent using the telephone system.

The functionality of user interaction has not been included in version 1.0 of the JCC specification in order to maintain separation of concerns. A separate Edit Group in JAIN is addressing user interaction. In combination with user interaction features many more services such as voice activated dialing, prepaid services, etc. can also be provided.

These services can be mapped into capabilities that must be made available via the API, and typically these capabilities are also required for numerous other applications. For example, VPN requires number look-up and translation capabilities during call set-up; this facility is also required for toll-free calls. CTD requires interaction between heterogeneous network types as well as voice/data integration.

Additional requirements defined for JCC include one that it support first-party as well as third-party call control. Here, as in JTAPI, a "first-party" call is one where the application or entity initiating the call is in control of a single address, whereas a "third-party" call is one where the application has control over two (or more) addresses. For example, a first-party call can be a call initiated directly by a user, using appropriate terminal equipment, via underlying signaling protocols appropriate for the network the user is connected to. On the other hand, a third-party call could be a situation where an application program initiates a call to connect two (or more) users or end devices. Hence, in the case of the third-party scenario an application has control over and can interact with more than one endpoint simultaneously. An example is a hotel wake-up call service, where the application program rings the guest's phone and connects him or her to an operator or automatic playback device.

In general JCC will also be required to support most of the features available as AIN or switch-based features in the PSTN, such as call forwarding, call waiting, etc. In addition, it is explicitly a requirement to keep the JCC API in harmony with existing Java APIs for call control, in particular JTAPI (e.g. allowing third-party call control using mechanisms similar to JTAPI.)

3.3.2 Basic components of the API

In this section we describe the basic objects of the API common to both JCP and JCC as well as the common design patterns to both packages.

For both JCC and JCP, the API components consist of a related set of interfaces, classes, operations, events, capabilities, and exceptions. The API provides four key objects, which are common to JCP, JCC and more advanced packages. The four key objects are:

- **Provider**: represents the "window" through which an application views the call processing.
- **Call**: represents a call and is a dynamic "connection of physical and logical entities" that bring two or more endpoints together.
- **Address**: represents a logical endpoint (e.g. directory number or IP address).
- **Connection**: represents the dynamic relationship between a **Call** and an **Address**.

The relationship among these objects is depicted pictorially in Figure 3.3 for a two-party call. Multiple parties are represented – with no inherent limitations in the model – simply by additional **Connections** and **Addresses** associated with a **Call**. In traditional telephony parlance, this model is "symmetric" in that there is no fundamental distinction at the highest level between originating and terminating parties of a call, and is a "full" model in the sense that the application, in principle, has a view of all parties of the call. (Of course, depending upon the deployment scenario, this view might not be complete or accurate at all times.)

The purpose of a **Connection** object is to describe the relationship between a **Call**

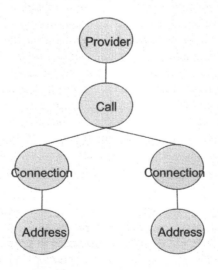

Figure 3.3 *Object model of a two-party call.*

object and an **Address** object. A **Connection** object exists if the **Address** is a part of the telephone call. **Connection** objects are immutable in terms of their **Call** and **Address** references. In other words, the **Call** and **Address** object references do not change throughout the lifetime of the **Connection** object instance. The same **Connection** object may not be used in another telephone call.

Basic API patterns: Listeners and Factories

The basic programming pattern of the API is that applications (which reside "above" the API) make synchronous calls to API methods, i.e. the application invoking the method blocks until the method completes processing and returns (Figure 3.4). The platform or network element implementing the API can inform the application of underlying events (e.g. the arrival of incoming calls) by means of Java events. The application provides **Listener** objects corresponding to the events that it is interested in obtaining.

In addition, the API also uses the Factory design pattern commonly used (and recommended) in Java. In brief, applications use a **PeerFactory** to obtain a **Peer**, which in Java nomenclature is "a particular platform-specific implementation of a Java interface or API", i.e. a vendor's particular implementation of the API. Applications then use the **Peer** to obtain access to the **Provider** object.

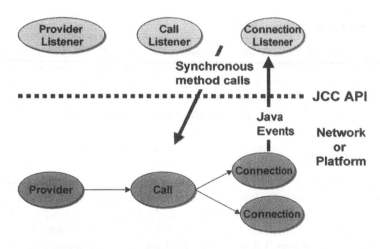

Figure 3.4   *API programming pattern using Java Listeners.*

Event and Listener inheritance diagrams

Since several objects in the API can generate events, which in turn can be trapped by different **Listeners** written by the application programmer, the **Event** and **Listener** objects are organized by inheritance. The inheritance diagrams are shown in Figure 3.5. The **ProviderEvent** indicates any state change occurring in

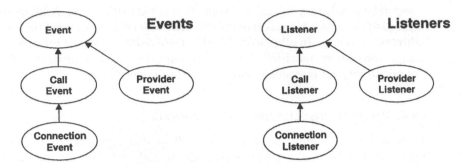

Figure 3.5 *JCC and JCP Event and Listener inheritance diagrams.*

the **Provider**, the **CallEvent** indicates state changes occurring in the **Call** object while the **ConnectionEvent** indicates state changes in the **Connection** object. These events are in turn reported to their corresponding listeners namely the **ProviderEvent** to the **ProviderListener**, the **CallEvent** to the **CallListener** and the **ConnectionEvent** to the **ConnectionListener**. Further a **ConnectionEvent** inherits from a **CallEvent** while the **ConnectionListener** inherits from a **CallListener**.

3.3.3 Java call processing (JCP)

In this section we describe the basic components of JCP. JCP is the elementary Java package from which more advanced call control packages inherit. JCP provides, among others, a few key methods to support its primary features of monitoring calls. The JCP specification defines, for each method, the pre- and post-conditions of the method in terms of state transitions in these FSMs.

JcpProvider

A **JcpProvider** represents the software-entity that interfaces with a telephony subsystem. The telephony subsystem could be a PBX connected to a server machine, a telephony/fax card in a desktop machine or a networking technology such as IP or ATM. The **JcpProvider** object has a state machine associated with it as shown in Figure 3.6. For the **Provider** FSM, the meanings of the states are as follows.

- IN_SERVICE: this state indicates that the **Provider** is currently alive and available for use.
- OUT_OF_SERVICE: this state indicates that a **Provider** is temporarily not available for use. Many methods in this API are invalid when the **Provider** is in this state. **Providers** may come back in service at any time; however, the application can take no direct action to cause this change.

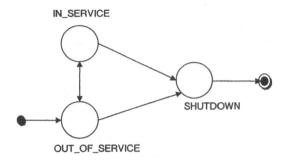

IN_SERVICE

SHUTDOWN

OUT_OF_SERVICE

Figure 3.6 *JCP and JCC Provider FSM.*

- SHUTDOWN: this state indicates that a **Provider** is permanently no longer available for use. Most methods in the API are invalid when the **Provider** is in this state. Applications have access to a method to cause a **Provider** to move into the SHUTDOWN state.

A **Provider** is the entity that a call control application has to access in order to initiate the placement of a call. An incoming signal into a platform also contacts the **Provider** initially before any further action can take place. An application does not create a **JcpProvider** object directly but obtains access to one using the getProvider() method in the *JcpPeer* interface.

Since JCP is an elementary package that maintains the commonality between JTAPI and JCC, the **JcpProvider** has a very primitive behavior. The behavior is evidenced by the methods on the **JcpProvider**. The **JcpProvider** has methods to allow the addition and deletion of the listeners on the **Provider**, to obtain the name and state of the **JcpProvider**, to shutdown the **JcpProvider**, to initiate a call by creating the **JcpCall** object as well as a method to return the object given an address string. Note that this object is expected to be a **JcpAddress** object corresponding to the address string given.

JcpCall

A **JcpCall** is a transient object representing communication between two or more parties. Invoking the createCall() method on the **JcpProvider** creates this object for an outgoing call. For an incoming call, the platform creates this call due to the incoming network signals. The call and its associated connection and address objects describe the control and media flows taking place in some underlying physical communication network. Note that in JCC 1.0 a call may be controlled by any of the parties involved in the call, not just the originating connection, thereby causing the membership and state of the endpoints of the call to change.

The **JcpCall** object represents an indirect relationship between the **JcpProvider** and the **JcpAddress** through the **JcpConnection**. (We will look at these other

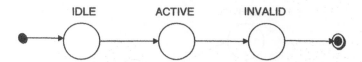

IDLE   ACTIVE   INVALID

Figure 3.7 *JCP Call object FSM.*

objects later.) The **JcpCall** maintains a reference to its **JcpProvider** for the life of that **JcpCall** object. The **JcpProvider** object instance does not change throughout the lifetime of the **JcpCall** object. The **JcpProvider** associated with a **JcpCall** is obtained via the getProvider() method on the **JcpCall** object.

The **JcpCall** object has a state machine associated with it as shown in Figure 3.7. For the **JcpCall** FSM, the meanings of the states are as follows.

- IDLE: this is the state in which all calls begin. In this state, the **JcpCall** does not have any **JcpConnections** associated with it.

- ACTIVE: a call with some current ongoing activity is in this state. In this state the **JcpCall** object must have one or more associated **JcpConnections**.

- INVALID: this is the final state for any **JcpCall** object. In this state the **JcpCall** object must have zero **JcpConnections** associated with it. Further, a **JcpCall** object in this state may not be used for any future action.

The **JcpCall** object has five methods associated with it. Three of these methods are used to provide information about the **JcpProvider** associated with the **JcpCall**, the state of the **JcpCall** as well as the **JcpConnections** associated with this **JcpCall**. The other two methods exist in order to add and remove call listeners on the **JcpCall** object.

JcpConnection

A **JcpConnection** object describes the relationship between a **JcpCall** object and a **JcpAddress** object. This is also transient in that the object exists only as long as this connection on the call exists. Hence, a new **JcpConnection** object has to be created for every new connection that has to be set up on a call.

Each **JcpConnection** has a state that describes the particular stage of the relationship between the **JcpCall** and **JcpAddress** (Figure 3.8). These states and their meanings as taken from the JCC specification are given below. Note the intentional similarity between this FSM and the FSM for the **Connection** object of the JTAPI Core API.

- IDLE: this state is the initial state for all new **Connections**. **Connections** in the IDLE state are not actively part of a call, yet their references to the **Call** and

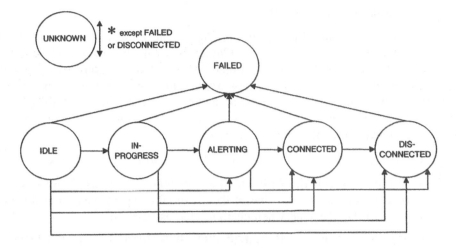

Figure 3.8 *JCP Connection object FSM.*

Address objects are valid. **Connections** typically do not stay in the IDLE state for long, quickly transitioning to other states.

- DISCONNECTED: this state implies that the connection is no longer part of the call, although its references to **Call** and **Address** still remain valid. A **Connection** in this state is interpreted as once previously belonging to this call.

- INPROGRESS: this state implies that the connection object has been contacted by the origination side or is contacting the destination side. The contact happens as a result of the underlying protocol messages. Extension packages elaborate further on this state in various situations.

- ALERTING: this state implies that the **Address** is being notified of an incoming call.

- CONNECTED: this state implies that a **Connection** and its **Address** are actively part of a call. In common terms, two people talking to one another are represented by two **Connections** in the CONNECTED state.

- UNKNOWN: this state implies that the implementation is unable to determine the current state of the **Connection**. Typically, methods are invalid on **Connections** that are in this state. **Connections** may move in and out of the UNKNOWN state at any time.

- FAILED: this state indicates that a **Connection** to that end of the call has failed for some reason. One reason why a **Connection** would be in the FAILED state is because the party was busy.

Three methods exist on the *JcpConnection* interface. These are used to obtain information about the **JcpAddress** and **JcpCall** associated with the **JcpConnection** as well as a method to obtain the state of the JcpConnection object.

Immutable connections

A **JcpConnection** object is *immutable*, in the sense that over the lifetime of a **JcpConnection** object, the **JcpConnection** can be associated with only one **JcpCall** and one **JcpAddress** object. If any of these (**JcpCall** or **JcpAddress**) objects have to be changed a new **JcpConnection** object has to be created. Note that this implies that every time an address associated with a **JcpConnection** has to change such as in the case of call forwarding, redirection, etc. a new **JcpConnection** object has to be created.

The advantages of having an immutable **JcpConnection** are as follows:

- Simpler FSM. If the **Call** and **Address** objects associated with a **Connection** object were allowed to change then it should be possible to transition from any state to the idle state when changing the association.

- No additional events. If the **JcpConnection** object were mutable then additional events (such as ending address/call association, starting address/call association) would be required to let the application know when the association between the connection and the **JcpCall** or the **JcpAddress** object (or both) changes.

The disadvantages of having an immutable **JcpConnection** are as follows:

- Additional **Connection** object management effort. With immutable connections some extra effort is required in the creation and management of **Connection** objects. For example, consider party A calling party B and assume that the call has to be redirected to C. With immutable **Connections**, initially two **JccConnections** will exist at B (one modeling the terminating connection from A and the other modeling the originating connection to C), which would be merged and/or deleted once the call set-up to C completes. On the other hand, with mutable **Connections** only one **JccConnection** need exist at B. Of course, this single **JccConnection** will need to have information about the originating party A. This is so that the association between the redirected party and the originating party can be made for the purpose of setting up the data path. When the call ends none of these **JccConnections** need be destroyed but could be reused. (Note, however, that this latter effect, i.e. object reuse, can be obtained by object pooling and is an implementation issue rather than a modeling issue. In fact, one could argue that the reuse of objects should not be made visible at the API level in order to free the programmer from object management chores and to allow the programmer a more abstract view of call processing.)

The issue of connection mutability was discussed extensively within the JCC Edit Group, and it was decided that on balance immutable connections were preferable. This is also in keeping with the practical experience of the JTAPI community.

JcpAddress

A **JcpAddress** is an object that represents an endpoint in a communication. This can represent a telephone number, e-mail address, etc. Every **JcpAddress** object is expected to have a corresponding string representation, which for example can be the telephone number. During the course of communication between two or more parties, address objects are related to **Call** objects via the **Connection** object. The state of the **Connection** object describes the current relationship between the **Call** and the **Address**. Each address object may be part of more than one call, and in each case, is represented by a separate **Connection** object.

Since the endpoints of a call are not transient, the **JcpAddress** objects, which represent these endpoints, are also not transient. Further, any **JcpAddress** object is expected to belong to the domain of some **JcpProvider**. Thus, every **JcpAddress** object has to have a **JcpProvider** associated with it. Based on this, relative to a given **JcpProvider** two types of **JcpAddresses** are possible, namely local and remote. A **JcpAddress** is considered local relative to a given **JcpProvider** if it belongs to the **JcpProvider's** domain and considered remote otherwise.

The methods on a *JcpAddress* interface are very primitive and are used to obtain the name of the **JcpAddress** object and the **JcpProvider** object associated with the **JcpAddress** object. Note that the name of the **JcpAddress** object is expected to be the same as its string representation.

3.3.4 Java call control (JCC)

In this section we look at JCC. The JCC API has the same four key objects as JCP, namely **Provider**, **Call**, **Connection** and **Address**. Since JCC inherits from JCP, each object may contain additional methods beyond those in JCP. We note that as for JCP, JCC **Connection** objects are immutable in terms of their **Call** and **Address** references. In other words, the **Call** and **Address** object references do not change throughout the lifetime of the **Connection** object instance. Note that the corresponding objects now have the Jcc prefix such as **JccCall**, **JccConnection**, etc.

JccProvider

The *JccProvider* interface inherits from the *JcpProvider* interface. An important feature exhibited by the *JccProvider* not provided by *JcpProvider* is the ability to act as a factory for **EventFilter** objects. The function of **EventFilter** objects is to act as a filtering mechanism for **Events**. We will look at **EventFilters** in detail later. The other methods on the **JccProvider** allow the ability to add listeners to the various call control objects in order to detect state changes in these objects.

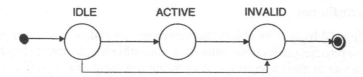

Figure 3.9 *JCC Call object FSM.*

JccCall

The *JccCall* interface inherits from the *JcpCall* interface. The states of the finite state machine are the same in case of both the interfaces, but the **JccCall** object has an extra transition visible to the application[4]. The JCC **Call** object FSM is shown in Figure 3.9.

The *JccCall* interface exhibits additional behavior as compared to a *JcpCall* interface. Some of the important methods are createConnection(), routeCall() and release(). We next consider these methods briefly. As explained earlier, a **JcpCall** and hence a **JccCall** represent a call. A call in turn consists of many connections.

In both JCC and JCP, an application wishing to initiate a call has to first create the object representing the call. This is achieved by invoking the createCall() method on the **JccProvider** interface. Note that a **JcpCall** object is returned by the JccProvider.createCall() method and this has to be cast to a **JccCall** object. The next step is to create the connections on the object representing the call by invoking the createConnection() method on the **JccCall** object. This method results in a new **JccConnection** object being created and associated with the **JccCall** and a given **JccAddress** object. First-party calls, third-party calls, call translation as well as call redirection can all be achieved by using different semantics associated with this method. In order to complete the call it has to be routed to the endpoint. This can be achieved by invoking the routeConnection() method on the **JccConnection** object. We will consider this method later while discussing the **JccConnection** interface.

The createConnection() method discussed above is used just to create a **JccConnection** object. The routeCall() method differs from the createConnection() method in that it not only creates a **JccConnection** object but also results in the JCC implementation initiating signaling in the network towards the endpoints of the call. Thus, the successful invocation of the routeCall() method results in the call having been successfully routed to an endpoint. This method can be used for first party calls, third party calls, number

---

[4] It might appear that we have a violation of the inheritance contract here. This discussion is outside the scope of this chapter. However, we point out briefly that one consistent view is that the underlying FSM for JcpCall is fully connected but the API only exposes a subset of the transitions. Subsequently, JccCall does not add any transitions, but chooses to expose an additional transition.

translation as well as call redirection. The `release()` method is used in order to release the call thereby freeing up the resources used up in the network. This will cause the **JccCall** and the corresponding **JccConnection** objects to be destroyed.

JccConnection

The *JccConnection* interface inherits from the *JcpConnection* interface. The important methods on a *JccConnection* interface are `routeConnection()`, `answer()`, `release()`, `continueProcessing()`, `getXXXAddress()`, `reDialedDigits()` and `selectRoute()`.

The **JccConnection** object has a different FSM from JCP. Note, however, that the JCC **Connection** FSM is a refinement of the JCP **Connection** FSM (i.e. obtained by adding transitions or splitting states into multiple states). In particular, the states of the **JccConnection** FSM map in a one-to-one fashion with the states of the **JcpConnection** FSM except for the INPROGRESS and CONNECTED states of the **JcpConnection** FSM. These two states are divided into further substates in

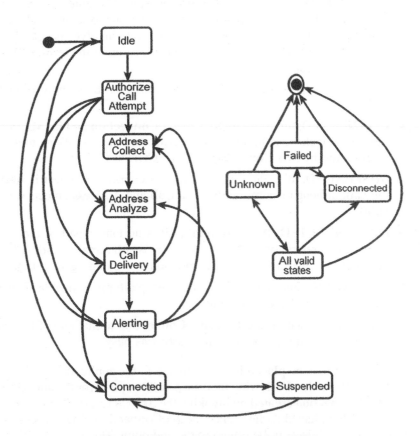

Figure 3.10 *JCC Connection object FSM.*

the **JccConnection** FSM. The FSM is shown in Figure 3.10. The states are described as:

- IDLE: this state is the initial state for all new **Connections**. Such **Connections** are not actively part of a telephone call, yet their references to the **Call** and **Address** objects are valid. **Connections** typically do not stay in the IDLE state for long, quickly transitioning to other states.

- AUTHORIZE_CALL_ATTEMPT: this state implies that the originating or terminating terminal needs to be authorized for the **Call**.

- ADDRESS_COLLECT: in this state the initial information package is collected from the originating party and is examined according to the "dialing plan" to determine the end of collection of addressing information.

- ADDRESS_ANALYZE: this state is entered on the availability of complete initial information package/dialing string from the originating party. The information collected is analyzed and/or translated according to a dialing plan to determine routing address and call type.

- CALL_DELIVERY: on the originating side this state involves selecting the route as well as sending an indication of the desire to set up a call to the specified called party. On the terminating side this state involves checking the busy/idle status of the terminating access and also informing the terminating message of an incoming call.

- ALERTING: this state implies that the **Address** is being notified of an incoming call.

- CONNECTED: this state implies that a **Connection** and its **Address** is actively part of a telephone call. In common terms, two parties talking to one another are represented by two **Connections** in the CONNECTED state.

- SUSPENDED: this state implies that this connection object is suspended from the call, although it's references to a **Call** and **Address** objects will still remain valid.

- DISCONNECTED: this state implies it is no longer part of the telephone call, although its references to **Call** and **Address** still remain valid. A **Connection** in this state is interpreted as once previously belonging to this telephone call.

- UNKNOWN: this state implies that the platform is unable to determine the current state of the **Connection**.

- FAILED: this state indicates that a **Connection** to that end of the call has failed for some reason (e.g. because the party was busy).

When a call is to be placed by an application, the application creates a call object using the **Provider**. Following this one possible option for the application is to have the **JccConnection** created by invoking the `JccCall.createConnection()` method, as explained earlier. Once the **JccConnection** object has been created, the connection will have to be routed to the end point. This is accomplished by invoking the `routeConnection()` method on the *JccConnection* interface. As a result of this the implementation causes signaling messages to be sent out over the network if necessary (unless both the originating and destination end point are on the same JCC platform). The destination party answers the incoming call by invoking the `answer()` method. When either party wishes to disconnect the call, it invokes the `release()` method on the corresponding **JccConnection** object. For a two-party call, the whole call is torn down when one of the parties hangs up; otherwise, the `release()` method on the **JccConnection** results in only the corresponding leg of the call being disconnected. The rest of the call may proceed with the reduced number of parties.

The method `selectRoute()` is intended to enable address translation. For example if A makes a toll-free call (where the destination number has a 1-800 prefix), the destination number will have to be translated to a routable number. The number translation application (registered beforehand as a listener) translates the number and returns control to the platform using the `selectRoute()` method. The method `getMoreDialedDigits()` is used by the application to instruct the platform to collect further address information (which may be in the form of digits or letters) and return this to the application. The platform is then expected to return only the additional information collected as a String. We will describe the `continueProcessing` method later in this same section when we discuss events.

Events and event blocking

As described earlier the finite state machine of the **JccConnection** object is a refinement of the finite state machine of the **JcpConnection** object. Further, every state transition results in an event being generated and reported to the registered listeners. The states of the **JccConnection** FSM map in a one-to-one fashion with the states of the **JcpConnection** FSM except for the INPROGRESS and CONNECTED states of the **JcpConnection** FSM. These two states are divided into further substates in the **JccConnection** FSM. Hence, it is expected that when the **JccConnection** object transitions from IDLE to AUTHORIZE_CALL_ATTEMPT, then two events are generated in the JCC platform corresponding to the INPROGRESS event and the AUTHORIZE_CALL_ATTEMPT. Two events are similarly generated when entering the CONNECTED state in the **JccConnection** FSM. On the other hand proceeding from one refined state to another refined state results in only the event corresponding to the destination state being generated. We would like to remark here that in order to determine the events to be delivered to the registered listeners we make use of the concept of **EventFilters** discussed later.

JccConnection object events can be reported to the listeners in either the blocking mode or the non-blocking mode. When an event occurs in the blocking mode the JCC implementation is required to suspend processing the call. In particular, further traversal of the finite state machine by the corresponding **JccConnection** object is suspended. However, all external events received (e.g. an indication that the other party has disconnected the call) for the blocked **JccConnection** object are queued and handled later by the **JccConnection** when call processing resumes. For a blocking event, the implementation must suspend processing either until the application uses a valid API method call or until a timeout occurs. The `continueProcessing()` method is one such method that the application can invoke to instruct the platform to continue call processing. This mode thus models triggers required by AIN services. Hence, events fired in the blocking mode can also be referred to as triggers. In the non-blocking mode the JCC implementation notifies the registered listeners of the event without suspending call processing. Note that the events on all other interfaces other than on the **JccConnection** interface are always reported in the non-blocking mode.

We remark here that feature interaction problems in the form of conflicting instructions resulting from a trigger can arise at this point. This complex problem is not solved by the JCC API and is outside the scope of the API. It is assumed that feature interaction is managed at the application level, or by means of provisioning and management functions that may determine, for instance, which applications may register for the same trigger and their relative priority. The JAIN SLEE may also provide facilities for managing feature interactions.

JCC Address

The *JccAddress* interface extends the *JcpAddress* interface. In JCC 1.0 the *JccAddress* provides only one method to obtain the type of the address. The type of address could be IP, E164, URL, etc.

Event Filters

The purpose of the *EventFilter* interface is to allow flexibility to the applications in specifying the events that the listener (and thereby the application if the application implements the listener interfaces or has a separate channel of communication with the listener) is interested in receiving from the JCC platform. This facility is important to minimize the performance penalty of events, particularly when the application interacts with the JCC platform across a network.

On the occurrence of an event, the JCC platform consults the *EventFilter* to determine whether any listeners should be notified of the event or not. In case no listener need be notified of the event, then the event is discarded. Otherwise, the appropriate listeners are notified of the event. Further, if the event is related to the *JccConnection* interface, the platform determines whether the event is to be reported in a blocking mode, and if so, suspends further FSM processing for that *JccConnection*.

There are two types of event filters: Customized event filters and Standard event filters. Customized event filters are objects created by applications and references which are supplied to the event source using the appropriate `addxxxListener()`

methods. While customized event filters are extremely flexible they can incur a significant performance penalty since the platform must essentially invoke a method on an object supplied by the application whenever an event occurs; this is particularly costly if the invocation occurs across a network.

Standard event filters are created by the JCC platform upon request by the application when the application invokes the appropriate `createEventFilterXXX()` method on the **JccProvider**. Standard event filters are expected to incur significantly less performance penalties than customized filters because they are executed on the same platform (and the same JVM) as the JCC implementation, and because the JCC implementation can use whatever techniques are necessary and appropriate to optimize their performance. Different standard event filters which can filter based on the addresses, based on **Provider**, **Call** or **Connection** based events or any combination of these can easily be created using the appropriate create methods on the **JccProvider**. Since these event filters are provided by the JCC platform they are not completely flexible but are expected to cater to the requirements of a majority of JCC applications.

3.4 Call flows

In this section we use message sequence charts (or "call flows") to illustrate the behavior of some selected applications. The goal is to illustrate typical sequences based on the current version of the JCC specification, which the application programmer might use in order to provide the named service. We illustrate two applications, one for the simple case where a first-party call is placed using the API, and the second for a much more complex situation where an application is monitoring and logging call activity. Further examples are given in the Call Flow document available in conjunction with the API specification itself.

Messages signaled between objects are shown as numbered lines with arrows indicating the direction of the signal. The messages are ordered temporally and the sequence number indicates this ordering. The objects that implement the interfaces are given at the top of each call flow. Note that the objects are normally identified based on the interfaces that they implement. Each message reflects the operation name to be invoked by the object, which receives the message. The messages are of two types, namely API messages and non-API messages. API messages are the messages flowing between objects representing the application and the objects representing the JCC platform. These are part of the specification. For the purpose of clarity we also show message flows between the different internal interfaces of the specification or between the different services in the application layer, which are the non-API messages. These non-API messages are implementation specific.

In Figures 3.11–3.13 AppLogic refers to the Application Logic (or application program). The application developer is also expected to provide an implementation of the relevant **Listener** classes (**JcpProviderListener**, **JcpCallListener**,

JcpConnectionListener, etc.) that the application expects to use. Normally, we show only the **JccConnectionListener** since we assume that in our call flows the application would need the services of only the **JccConnectionListener**. Recall that the **JccConnectionListener** is a subclass of **JccCallListener**. The objects provided by the JCC implementation are the **JccProvider**, **JccCall**, **JccConnection** and the **JccAddress** objects. In the call flows we may show only some of these objects to avoid cluttering the diagrams.

3.4.1 First-party call

We first show a call flow corresponding to an application at an endpoint originating a call. There are two parties on the call once it is established. Note that a similar call

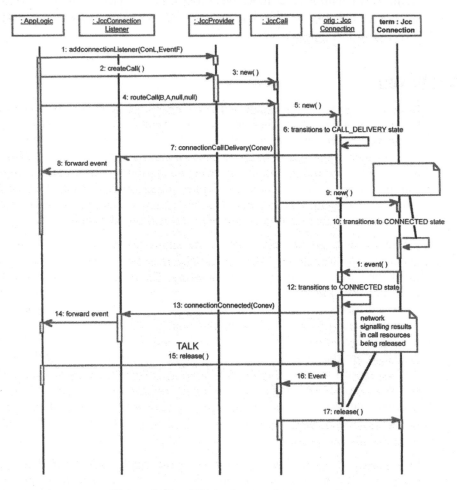

Figure 3.11   *JCC Application first party call.*

flow is also provided along with the JCC 1.0 specification. We ignore event filters in this call flow so as to keep the flow simple. In the next call flow, we look at the use of event filters in detail.

1. The application representing party A and denoted by AppLogic adds a listener **ConL** to the call with **EventF** denoting the **EventFilter**. The **EventFilter** is an object provided by the application that implements the **EventFilter** interface. Note that the application can use the addCallListener(call Listener) method if it desires to receive all events on all addresses associated with this **JccProvider**. (This is permitted since the *JccConnectionListener* interface extends the *JccCallListener* interface.) Note also that this method is equivalent to JccProvider.addCallListener(ConL, EventF) since parameter **ConL** is a **JcpConnectionListener** and hence also a **JcpCallListener**.

2. The application requests the **JccProvider** to create an object implementing the *JccCall* interface. A new instance of the call with no connections is created. The new **Call** object is in the IDLE state. An exception is generated if a new call cannot be created for any reason. For instance, the precondition for this method is that the **JccProvider** must be in the IN_SERVICE state, otherwise an InvalidStateException is thrown.

3. The **JccProvider** creates an object implementing the *JccCall* interface.

4. The application, representing party A, instructs the **JccCall** object to create a **JccConnection** object representing the originating party A and route the call to the destination party B. Routing the call to the destination party necessitates the creation of another **JccConnection** object associated with the destination address.

5. An object implementing the *JccConnection* interface representing the originating party A is created. Hereafter we refer to this **JccConnection** object as the originating **JccConnection**. Note that the getAddress() method invoked on this object returns a **JcpAddress** corresponding to the party A. Further, the getDestinationAddress() method invoked on this object returns a **JcpAddress** corresponding to party B. The **JccConnection** passes through different states while proceeding with the different steps of basic call processing such as authorizing whether a call with the given number can be set up (AUTHORIZE_CALL_ATTEMPT), analyzing the digits dialed for special processing such as on 1-800 calls or whether additional digits are required to complete the destination address (ADDRESS_ANALYZE).

6. This results in the **JccConnection** object transitioning to the CALL_DELIVERY state.

7. The registered **JccConnectionListener** is then informed of the originating **JccConnection** being in the CALL_DELIVERY state. This is done by sending an appropriate **JccConnectionEvent** using the connectionCall

`Delivery (connectionevent)` method that has to be implemented by the registered **JccConnectionListener object**.

8. The **JccConnectionListener** then informs the application about the occurrence of the event specified.

9. Since the implementation already has the address of the destination party B, it proceeds with the creation of a new **JccConnection** object representing B hereafter referred to as the terminating **JccConnection**. Note that the `getAddress()` method invoked on this terminating **JccConnection** object returns a **JcpAddress** corresponding to party B.

10. The terminating **JccConnection** object transits to the CONNECTED state possibly as a result of underlying network signaling. Note that many intervening events such as the alerting of the destination party, etc. have not been shown. Typically, the terminating **JccConnection** object passes through AUTHORIZE_CALL_ATTEMPT, CALL_DELIVERY and ALERTING states before transitioning to the CONNECTED state.

11. An event internal to the implementation then informs the originating **JccConnection** that the destination terminating **JccConnection** is in the CONNECTED state. Note that this way of informing the originating **JccConnection** is implementation specific and is not governed in any way by the API specification.

12. The originating **JccConnection** object transits to the CONNECTED state.

13. The JCC implementation then informs the **JccConnectionListener** that the original **JccConnection** representing party A is in the CONNECTED state.

14. The application is then informed of the originating **JccConnection** being in the CONNECTED state by the **JccConnectionListener**.

15. When the application decides to end the conversation, it does so by using this message on the originating **JccConnection**. This results in the originating **JccConnection** transitioning from the CONNECTED state to the DISCONNECTED state. Call resources related to the originating party may also be released on account of network signaling. Note also that this is one possible way in which the call may be released. There are other ways in which the call can be disconnected and which are not shown here. Additional **JccConnections** may be dropped indirectly as a result of this method. For example, dropping the destination **JccConnection** of a two-party call as shown here may result in the entire telephone call being dropped. It is up to the implementation to determine which **JccConnections** are dropped as a result of this method. Implementations should not, however, drop additional **JccConnections** representing additional parties if it does not reflect the natural response of the underlying telephone hardware.

16. Since there are only two parties in this call, this also results in the other party namely the terminating **JccConnection** also transitioning to the DISCONNECTED state. This is caused by this event sent internally within

the JCC implementation. Note that the way events are passed around classes is highly implementation specific.

17. This message causes the terminating **JccConnection** to transition to the DISCONNECTED state and call resources related to the destination party used up in the network are also released as a result of network signaling.

3.4.2 A call logging application

The application that we consider is a call logging application. This application maintains a record of the duration of the inbound calls to a particular address. In addition the application also blocks the call if certain criteria are satisfied. These criteria could be on the calling party so that calls from certain parties are not allowed for selective periods of time or the criteria could be based on the time of the day. Hence, this application has to be invoked every time a new call comes in and also before the connection is disconnected. Note that the logging application is notified of the call beginning and ending using a blocking event. Further, at the start of a connection if the logging application does not block the call and thereby disconnect it, it is handled by a regular application denoted as EndApp. Thus the EndApp application's function is assumed to be to answer calls.

In the call flows below we show an entity called the Dispatcher. All applications are expected to register all the events they are interested in with the Dispatcher. The Dispatcher is not mentioned or specified in the JCC API specification as it is not implemented by the JCC platform and it is not essential. However, we use the Dispatcher object in the following call flows to allow feature interaction problems to be resolved. Recall that the JCC platform does not explicitly provide any facilities to solve the problem of feature interaction. In this section we first describe how the call logging application can be implemented using customized event filters, and then using standard event filters.

Using customized event filters

We next describe briefly each of the steps involved in the call flow.

1. This message is used by the EndApp to register with the Dispatcher. The EndApp is also expected to notify the Dispatcher of its interest in receiving the alerting events for a certain range of addresses that it is responsible for. These details would depend on the API allowed by the Dispatcher for registration purposes.

2. We next show the CallLogApp also registering with the Dispatcher for the CONNECTION CREATED and the CONNECTION DISCONNECTED events. Note that we again skip showing details such as addresses and the events. For simplicity we also show the CallLogApp registering right after the basic application has registered.

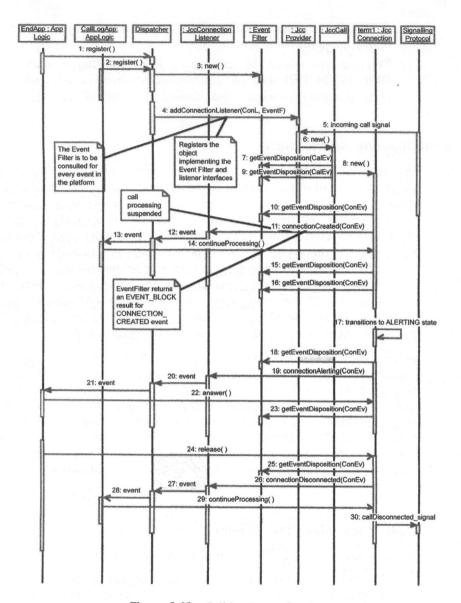

Figure 3.12 *Call logging application.*

3. This message is used by the Dispatcher to create an object implementing the *EventFilter* interface. Note that we show this message explicitly in this case only to bring attention to the fact that the object implementing the *EventFilter* interface in this case has to be provided *to* the JCC platform. This is in contrast to the next call flow where standard *EventFilter* interfaces are used and which are provided by the platform.

4. The Dispatcher then uses this message to register the **JccConnectionListener** object and the **EventFilter** objects with the JCC implementation. Note that based on the earlier explanation the **EventFilter** object registered by the Dispatcher is expected to contain the logic to return EVENT_BLOCK for the CONNECTION_CREATED and the CONNECTION_DISCONNECTED events while it returns EVENT_NOTIFY for the ALERTING event. We assume that the Dispatcher then does further demultiplexing of the events so that the appropriate application is notified.

5. This message is used to inform the **JccProvider** of an incoming call. Note that the underlying network-signaling protocols are responsible for the generation of this message.

6. An object implementing the *JccCall* interface is then created to model the incoming call by the JCC platform.

7. This message shows the **EventFilter** being consulted for the CALL_ CREATED event. This is because the intention of providing the **EventFilter** is that the JCC platform consults it on the occurrence of every event for indication of how the event is to be processed (block, notify, discard). It is assumed that the **EventFilter** returns EVENT_DISCARD.

8. An object implementing the **JccConnection** interface is then created to model the incoming connection.

9. Since a **JccConnection** object has been created, the **JccCall** object transitions to the ACTIVE state. Hence, the JCC platform consults the **EventFilter** for the disposition of the resulting CALL_ACTIVE event. It is assumed that the **EventFilter** returns EVENT_DISCARD.

10. This message shows the JCC platform consulting the **EventFilter** for another event, which is the CONNECTION_CREATED event. The **EventFilter** returns EVENT_BLOCK.

11. Since the **EventFilter** returned EVENT_BLOCK the `connection Created()` method is invoked on the registered **JccConnectionListener**. Note also that call processing is blocked as a result.

12. The **JccConnectionListener** then notifies the Dispatcher of the occurrence of the CALL_CREATED event.

13. The Dispatcher then forwards this event to the CallLogging application based on the earlier registration.

14. The CallLogging application notes down the time of the start of the call and checks whether the call should be allowed to proceed or whether it should be disconnected. In this case we assume that the call is allowed to proceed and hence the CallLogging application then invokes the `continueProces sing()` method on the blocked **JccConnection** object to cause resumption of call processing.

15. Since call processing is resumed the **JccConnection** transitions to the AUTHORIZE_CALL_ATTEMPT state. Therefore, the JCC platform consults the **EventFilter** for the resulting event. The **EventFilter** is assumed to return EVENT_DISCARD.

16. This message shows the platform consulting the **EventFilter** for another event namely CONNECTION_CALL_DELIVERY. The **EventFilter** returns EVENT_DISCARD. Note that this **JccConnection** transitioned from the AUTHORIZE_CALL_ATTEMPT to the CALL_DELIVERY state as it is a terminating connection.

17. This message indicates that the **JccConnection** has transitioned to the ALERTING state.

18. This message shows the platform consulting the **EventFilter** for the CONNECTION_ALERTING event. The **EventFilter** returns EVENT_ NOTIFY.

19. Since the **EventFilter** returned EVENT_NOTIFY, hence the `connection Alerting()` method is invoked on the registered **JccConnectionListener**. Note also that call processing is not suspended but the **JccConnection** object remains in the ALERTING state unless an `answer()` or `release()` method is invoked.

20. The **JccConnectionListener** then notifies the Dispatcher of the occurrence of the CALL_ALERTING event.

21. The Dispatcher then forwards this event to the application based on the earlier registration.

22. Since the application wants to answer the call, it invokes the `answer()` method on the **JccConnection** object. This results in the **JccConnection** object transitioning to the CONNECTED state.

23. Transitioning of the **JccConnection** object to the CONNECTED state results in the CONNECTION_CONNECTED event being generated. Hence, the JCC platform has to consult the **EventFilter** for disposition of this event. The EventFilter is assumed to return EVENT_DISCARD.

24. At the end of the communication, the EndApp application releases the call by invoking the `release()` API on the **JccConnection** object.

25. This results in the CONNECTION_DISCONNECTED event. The **Event Filter** is again consulted for the disposition of this event. The **EventFilter** returns EVENT_BLOCK.

26. Since the **EventFilter** returned EVENT_BLOCK, hence the `connection Disconnected()` method is invoked on the registered **JccConnection Listener**. Note also that call processing is blocked as a result.

27. The **JccConnectionListener** then notifies the Dispatcher of the occurrence of the CALL_DISCONNECTED event.

28. The Dispatcher then forwards this event to the CallLogging application based on the earlier registration.

29. The CallLogging application notes down the time of the end of the call and then invokes the `continueProcessing()` method on the blocked **JccConnection** object to cause the completion of call disconnection.

Using standard event filters

We next consider the call flow of the call logging application but using standard event filters.

1. This message is used by the EndApp to register with the Dispatcher. The EndApp is also expected to notify the Dispatcher of its interest in receiving the alerting events for a certain range of addresses that it is responsible for. These details would depend on the API allowed by the Dispatcher for registration purposes.

2. We next show the CallLogApp also registering with the Dispatcher for the CONNECTION CREATED and the CONNECTION DISCONNECTED

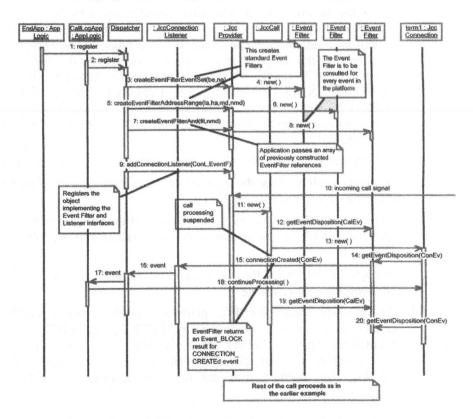

Figure 3.13 *Call logging application using standard event filters.*

events. Note that we again skip showing the relevant details such as addresses and the events. We also show the CallLogApp registering right after the basic application has registered for simplicity.

3. Standard **EventFilters** are to be provided by the platform. Hence, the Dispatcher uses this message to request the JCC platform to create an **EventFilter** object, which will filter events based on their types.

4. The new **EventFilter** object is then created by the platform.

5. The Dispatcher uses this message to request the JCC platform to create an **EventFilter** object, which will filter events based on the addresses associated with the events.

6. The new **EventFilter** is then created by the platform.

7. The Dispatcher then uses this message to request the platform to create an **EventFilter** object that will use both the previously created filters. Thus this will result in events being filtered based on the type AND the address.

8. The new **EventFilter** is then created by the platform.

9. The Dispatcher then uses this message to register the **JccConnectionListener** object and the combined **EventFilter** object (created in the previous step) with the JCC implementation. Note that based on the earlier explanation for the call blocking and the end application, the combined **EventFilter** object registered by the Dispatcher is expected to contain the logic to return EVENT_BLOCK for the CONNECTION_CREATED and the CONNEC-TION_DISCONNECTED events while it returns EVENT_NOTIFY for the ALERTING event for events occurring on the given address. The Dispatcher then does further demultiplexing of the events so that the appropriate application is notified.

10. This message is used to inform the **JccProvider** of an incoming call.

11. An object implementing the *JccCall* interface is then created to model the incoming call by the JCC platform.

12. This message shows the combined **EventFilter** being consulted for the CALL_CREATED event. It is assumed that the **EventFilter** returns EVENT_DISCARD.

13. An object implementing the *JccConnection* interface is then created to model the incoming connection.

14. This message shows the JCC platform consulting the **EventFilter** for another event, which is the CONNECTION_CREATED event. The **EventFilter** returns EVENT_BLOCK. Note that the CALL_ACTIVE event is shown to occur after this event in this call flow unlike the earlier call flow. This is to illustrate the fact that the order of events might be platform specific.

15. Since the **EventFilter** returned EVENT_BLOCK, hence the `connectionCreated()` method is invoked on the registered **JccConnectionListener**. Note also that call processing is blocked as a result.

16. The **JccConnectionListener** then notifies the Dispatcher of the occurrence of the CALL_CREATED event.

17. The Dispatcher then forwards this event to the CallLogging application.

18. The CallLogging application notes down the time of the start of the call and checks whether the call should be allowed to proceed or whether it should be disconnected. In this case, as earlier, we assume that the call is allowed to proceed and hence the CallLogging application then invokes the `continueProcessing()` method on the blocked **JccConnection** object to cause resumption of call processing.

19. The resumption of call processing then results in the CALL_ACTIVE event being generated. This happens since the **JccCall** object transitions to the ACTIVE state. Hence, the JCC platform consults the **EventFilter** for the disposition of the resulting CALL_ACTIVE event. It is assumed that the EventFilter returns EVENT_DISCARD.

20. The **JccConnection** transitions to the AUTHORIZE_CALL_ATTEMPT state. Therefore, the JCC platform consults the **EventFilter** for the resulting event. The **EventFilter** is assumed to return EVENT_DISCARD.

3.5 Discussion: JCC and its relationships to JAIN, JTAPI and Parlay

3.5.1 JCC and signaling protocols

We first discuss the relationship of JCC to the JAIN Protocols Expert Group. The JCC API provides the applications programmer with convenient, powerful, object-oriented abstractions for manipulating calls and managing the interaction between applications and calls. As such, a primary purpose of JCC is to hide the multiplicity of underlying signaling protocols used to set up, maintain, and tear down calls over heterogeneous networks. This is shown diagrammatically in Figure 3.14, where it is assumed that applications interact with the JCC API in order to avoid interacting with specific protocols.

Nonetheless, note that JAIN is in fact developing, or has already issued, Java APIs to all the signaling protocols shown in the figure, and more as can be seen from other chapters in this book. An application that wishes may access these underlying protocol APIs, bypassing the abstractions offered by JCC. An application that does so will typically get finer-grained control, as it can select, for example, the precise sequence and content of messages sent by the protocol. Bypassing the JCC layer may also have some performance advantages, in some cases, since the overhead of

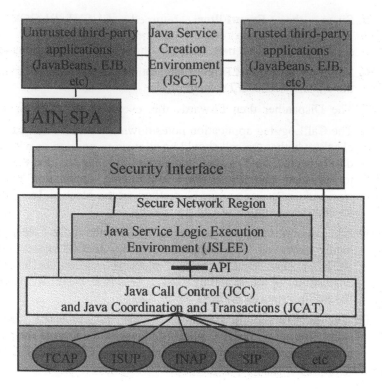

Figure 3.14 *Diagram depicting approximate relationships of JAIN edit groups.*

creating and manipulating the JCC objects is avoided. On the other hand, the applications programmer will be forced to deal with low-level details involved with each protocol (in terms of message and parameter types, etc.), and will not have the advantage of using the logical abstractions offered by JCC.

For example, to add a party to an existing call, the application programmer using JCC can simply invoke a single method, called, say, routeCall(), with the appropriate parameters. In contrast, using the protocol API, the application programmer would typically have to send and receive a sequence of protocol messages via the API. Thus, the time to develop and test applications will typically be reduced significantly by using JCC. In addition, using the JCC abstraction means that the application is independent of which underlying protocols are used, and which type of network the application is running on (IP, PSTN, or wireless). In this sense, bypassing JCC to develop applications directly using the protocol APIs is roughly analogous to developing applications in assembly language, for performance or other reasons, rather than using the abstractions offered by a high-level language like Java or C++.

3.5.2 JCC and application-level facilities

In order to provide the reader with an understanding of the work of the JCC Edit Group in the context of the overall service creation and execution process and the JAIN Applications Expert Group as a whole, we use the diagram shown in Figure 3.14. Note that this diagram is intended for illustration purposes only. It is not intended to necessarily be a software layering diagram. There have been numerous discussions within the JAIN AEG attempting to define the scope of each Edit Group and their inter-relationships. These relationships continue to evolve as different Edit Groups continue to iteratively refine their specifications and work efforts. *The diagram of Figure 3.14 and discussion in this section is intended to be purely illustrative; it is not a final formal position of JAIN or any particular Edit Group within JAIN.*

JCC and service development and execution

The JAIN AEG architecture is designed to allow access to the integrated network both for untrusted third-party applications as well as trusted (service-provider created or third-party) applications. Applications would typically be written using components like JavaBeans (JB) [13] or Enterprise JavaBeans (EJB) [14] and would be created using a Java Service Creation Environment (JSCE) and execute within a Java service logic execution environment (JSLEE). It is possible that third-party integrated development environments (IDE) will provide many of the facilities required in this area. The requirements and framework of the JSCE and JSLEE are within the scope of the JSCE and JSLEE Edit Groups.

Both untrusted and trusted applications must first undergo appropriate security checks before they can access the network resources made available via JCC. Note that these security checks may be needed to not only authenticate and authorize the applications to the network but also vice versa. Pictorially we have depicted the region where applications may execute after undergoing security checks as the "secure network region".

Note that in the diagram we show the JSLEE pictorially as residing between the applications and JCC. Obviously trusted applications would actually execute using the facilities of the JSLEE, which could act as a "container" in the EJB sense. In this sense trusted applications execute "inside" the JSLEE, which could then be represented as the entire secure network region, and in fact JCC as well as the underlying protocols reside inside the JSLEE. On the other hand, in the view of JCC, some applications may execute on a third-party SLEE different from that defined by the JSLEE Edit Group of JAIN. In the extreme case, the SLEE may simply be a minimalist environment consisting only of a Java virtual machine (JVM). As the JSLEE Edit Group evolves this precise relationship will be expanded and clarified.

Relationship of JCC to JAIN service provider API (SPA)

We now discuss the position of untrusted applications and the JAIN SPA API with respect to JCC. As mentioned above, trusted applications would typically execute inside the JSLEE. Untrusted applications may execute on third-party SLEEs (e.g. on enterprise applications servers or PBXs) outside the secure network region. It is envisioned that untrusted applications would utilize the APIs developed by the JAIN SPA Edit Group.

The JAIN SPA 1.0 API is based on the Parlay API 1.2 specification issued by the Parlay community, and is designed to allow untrusted applications access to network resources in a controlled and limited manner. As such, it contains strong facilities for authenticating and authorizing untrusted applications. (Note that in the view of JCC, untrusted applications must still go through a further layer of security, which is the same as for trusted applications, to access the JCC abstractions).

The Parlay API specification on which JAIN SPA is based also contains specifications for call control, as discussed below. However, it has been decided in the JAIN AEG that JCC is the standard call control API within JAIN and that call control specification is outside the scope of JAIN SPA. This was done to avoid duplication of effort and to ensure a single locus of alignment between JAIN and Parlay.

3.5.3 Relationship of JCC and JCP to JTAPI and Parlay APIs

The relationship between JCP, JCC and the call control APIs of JTAPI and Parlay is depicted pictorially via the object inheritance diagram in Figure 3.15.

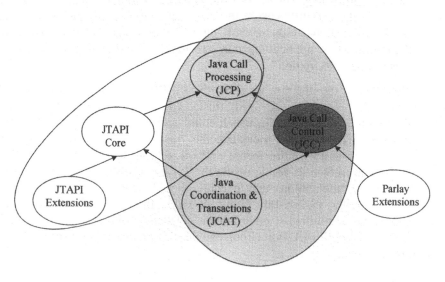

Figure 3.15 *Relationship of JCC packages to JTAPI and Parlay.*

The JCP package is an elementary call control package from which all other packages inherit. The left ellipse in the figure represents call control extensions for CTI type of applications, and consists of the JTAPI core package as well as its extensions. The central shaded ellipse represents the domain of call control packages defined by the JAIN consortium. In addition to JCP and JCC, it includes the JCAT package to be defined to provide advanced call control and IN/AIN type of functionality. Note though that the relationship of JCP to JTAPI as described here is only recommended and will have to be decided upon by the JTAPI group.

Finally, the Parlay extension packages (e.g. multimedia or conferencing) are intended to extend from JCC along the right side of the figure. JCC itself is based around the language-neutral Parlay 2.1 multi-party call control service (MPCCS) specification in an effort to harmonize JAIN and Parlay call control. (It is hoped that the gap between the language-neutral Parlay specification and JCC call control will be diminished as the two groups work together.) Note that for Java however, JCC is the official Java instantiation of Parlay call control.

Note that with this structure a programmer using JCP and JCC is linked closely to the other Java specifications for call control, namely JTAPI and the Java instantiation of Parlay call control. In particular, the objects, methods and programming paradigms of the JCP, JCC and JTAPI packages are closely related and consistent, so that a programmer who develops expertise and code for one is relevant to the others.

3.6 Concluding remarks

It is clear that future telecommunications networks will be integrated networks of packet-switched (ATM or IP) and circuit-switched networks and it is also clear that to provide the large portfolio of innovative services that service providers desire to offer in these networks, open network APIs will be required. A central component of these APIs will be the API for call control (initiating and manipulating calls) and coordination and transactions (invoking and executing services before or during calls). The JCC 1.0 API defines the standard Java API for call control and coordination and transactions. Given the growing popularity of Java for applications development, it is expected that the JCC API will be an important tool for rapid service development in future telecommunications networks.

At present the JCC 1.0 specification is available as a free download from the official JAIN website. It includes an overview article, a document describing example call flows, and the JavaDoc of the specification itself. In addition, Telcordia, as part of its Edit Lead responsibilities to the JAIN community, has implemented a reference implementation (RI) and test compatibility kit (TCK) that are also available to the Java community. The RI illustrates the feasibility of implementing the JCC 1.0 API and also serves as a simple test platform to allow programmers to test example JCC applications. The TCK illustrates the feasibility of writing useful applications to the

JCC API, and also serves as a test suite to allow platform implementers to test their implementation. (Note that the RI and TCK are not supported Telcordia products, come without warranty, and are intended to be preliminary test vehicles and not fully-fledged implementations or test suites for the JCC 1.0 API.)

We point out that there are numerous issues that still need to be addressed in the implementation of a platform that supports the JCC API. These include issues of performance and capacity planning; for instance how one would dimension such a call processing platform to meet desired performance objectives. Reliability and availability issues are also extremely important, and it is expected that testing would be a significant task. These issues are challenging for any high-volume, high-reliability call processing system, and addressing them adequately is similarly a challenge for any implementation of the JCC API.

Acknowledgements

The authors thank the individual experts of the JCC Edit Group for their participation in the definition of the JCC API. The support of the entire Sun JAIN team, in particular Margaret Nilson, Gary Bruce, and Doug Tait, is also gratefully acknowledged. Special thanks go to John-Luc Bakker, Paolo Missier, and Raman Shastry of Telcordia, all of who have contributed substantially at various times to the API specification. Special thanks also to Phil Ber for his comments as well as implementation of the JCC 1.0 RI and TCK. Thanks are due to Jim Garrahan and Surinder Jain of Telcordia for bringing their expertise, particularly on AIN and other API-related issues.

References

1. Anjum F, Caruso F, Jain R, Missier P, Zordan A. ChaiTime: a system for rapid creation of portable next-generation telephony services using third-party software components. Proc. IEEE Conf. Open Arch. Network Prog. (OPENARCH), March 1999.

2. Anjum F, Caruso F, Jain R, Missier P, Zordan A. CitiTime: a system for rapid creation of portable next-generation telephony services. Computer networks. Amsterdam, Elsevier, 2001 (in press).

3. Roberts S. Essential JTAPI. Englewood Cliffs, NJ, 1999, 555 pp.

4. Krupczak B, Calvert KL, Ammar MH. Implementing communication protocols in Java. IEEE Communications October 1998.

5. International Telecommunication Union. Visual telephone systems and equipment for local area networks which provide a non-guaranteed quality of service. Recommendation H.323,Telecommunication Standardization Sector of ITU, Geneva, Switzerland, May 1996.

6. Handley M, Schulzrinne H, Schooler E, Rosenberg J. SIP: session initiation protocol. Request for Comments (Proposed Standard) 2543, Internet Engineering Task Force, March 1999.

7. Russell T. Signaling System 7. New York: McGraw-Hill, 1998, 500 pp.

8. Black U. The intelligent network. Englewood Cliffs, NJ: Prentice-Hall, 1998, 208 pp.

9. Sun Microsystems. Java Telephony API v. 1.2 Specification, 1998. Available from http://java.sun.com/products/jtapi.

10. Microsoft. IP telephony with TAPI 3.0, white paper, December 1998. Available from http://www.microsoft.com/ISN/whitepapers/ip_telephony_with_ta.asp.

11. O'Reilly-Roche M. Call party handling using the connection view state approach: a foundation for intelligent control of multiparty calls. IEEE Communications, June 1998.

12. Farley J, Loukides M, editors. Java distributed computing. O'Reilly, Sebastopol, CA, 1998, 384 pp.

13. Englander R. Developing java beans. O'Reily, Sebastopol, CA, 1997, 316 pp.

14. Valesky T. Enterprise JavaBeans. Reading, MA: Addison-Wesley, 1999, 326 pp.

4

Realtime Java for telecommunications

Thomas C. Jepsen

Programming Languages Editor, IT Professional, USA

4.1 What is realtime programming?

Realtime programs are computer programs that must execute within pre-defined time constraints. Creating such programs requires special consideration to be given to timing and scheduling of operations, and allocation of physical resources. For example, realtime programs are intolerant of delayed execution, and often it is preferable to defer or deny execution than to allow the program to return a late response. Examples of telecommunications applications that require realtime programming are telephony circuit switching, voice synthesis, and multimedia presentation.

Two general types of realtime applications are defined. Hard realtime systems are systems in which early or late responses are not acceptable. A real world example of a hard realtime system is an air traffic control system; if airplanes were to be allowed to land or take off earlier or later than their scheduled departure times, there would be a risk of collision with other airplanes. Therefore a properly functioning air traffic control system will (1) deny an airplane permission to take off at a time outside of its scheduled departure time, and (2) re-schedule its departure for the next available safe time slot.

Another example of a hard realtime system is a multimedia frame display system. To properly display motion video, a new frame must be presented to the viewer at precisely timed intervals. Early or late display of frames will produce video of unacceptable quality.

Soft realtime systems, on the other hand, are tolerant of a certain amount of delay. A network packet router is a good example of a soft realtime system. For most data applications, it is better to send a packet late than to not send it at all. Transport control protocol over Internet protocol (TCP/IP) is a good example of a soft real-time protocol; it includes a retransmission capability that enables missing packets to be detected and re-transmitted, at the cost of additional transport latency.

Since realtime programs must operate within time constraints, special considerations are required. The programmer must calculate the processor and memory requirements for each operation and then determine the total system workload. The programmer must then use a scheduling method to determine priority of execution. A common technique is *rate monotonic scheduling*. In rate monotonic scheduling, task priority is assigned in the order of decreasing execution frequency. Tasks that execute most frequently are assigned the highest priority, and tasks that execute least often are assigned the lowest execution priority. A mathematical analysis can then be done to demonstrate that in a worst-case scenario, all tasks will complete before the end of the execution interval, given a certain CPU capacity. For rate monotonic scheduling, this is possible if the total workload is less than 69% of the total CPU capacity [1].

4.1.1 *Rationale for development of a realtime capability for Java*

Although Java was originally intended for use in embedded systems, it is not well suited for realtime applications without significant functional additions. The functions that give Java its ease of use and platform independence, namely garbage collection and the use of a virtual machine execution environment, make it difficult to control time- and resource-dependent operations. The fact that different operating systems have different methods of implementing thread priorities further complicates the issue.

The realtime specification for Java (RTSJ)

To address these and other issues related to realtime programming using Java, a number of individuals began work on realtime Java implementations in the late 1990s. Kelvin Nilsen of NewMonics, Lisa Carnahan from the National Institute for Standards and Technology (NIST), and Greg Bollella of IBM were joined by Kevin Russell and James Gosling of Sun Microsystems to form a realtime Java experts working group in 1998. In the same year, IBM asked Sun to accept a Java Specification Request for the development of a realtime specification for Java. The first draft of JSR-000001, *The Real Time Specification for Java*, was published for review by Java Community Process participants in September 1999. A proposed final draft version is now available on the Java Community Process website [2].

Guiding principles for the RTSJ

The following principles guided the development of the realtime specification for Java, and are taken from the specification itself:

- *Applicability to particular Java environments*: the realtime specification for Java shall not include specifications that restrict its use to particular Java environments (e.g. particular versions of the Java Development Kit, the Embedded Java Application Environment, or the Java 2 Platform, Micro Edition).

- *Backward compatibility*: the realtime specification for Java shall not prevent existing, properly written non-realtime Java programs from executing on implementations of the realtime specifications for Java.

- *Write once, run anywhere*: the realtime specification for Java should recognize the importance of "write once, run anywhere," (WORA) but it should also recognize the difficulty of achieving WORA for realtime programs and not attempt to increase or maintain binary portability at the expense of predictability.

- *Current practice vs. advanced features*: the realtime specification for Java should address current realtime system practice as well as allow future implementations to include advanced features.

- *Predictable execution*: the realtime specification for Java shall hold predictable execution as first priority in all tradeoffs; this may sometimes be at the expense of typical general-purpose computing performance measures.

- *No syntactic extension*: in order to facilitate the job of tool developers, and thus to increase the likelihood of timely implementations, the realtime specification for Java shall not introduce new keywords or make other syntactic extensions to the Java language.

- *Allow variation in implementation decisions*: The realtime Java experts group recognizes that implementations of the realtime specification for Java may vary in a number of implementation decisions, such as the use of efficient or inefficient algorithms, tradeoffs between time and space efficiency, inclusion of scheduling algorithms not required in the minimum implementation, and variation in code path length for the execution of byte codes. The realtime specification for Java should not mandate algorithms or specific time constants for such, but require that the semantics of the implementation be met. The realtime specification for Java offers implementers the flexibility to create implementations suited to meet the requirements of their customers.

4.2 Enhancements for realtime Java

The Real Time Java Experts Group determined that seven areas of the Java language required enhancements to support realtime programming; in addition, new exception classes specifically for realtime programming were defined. Each is described below.

4.2.1 Thread scheduling and dispatching

The Real Time Java Experts Group recognized that there are many scheduling and dispatching models used by different operating systems and runtime environments; they also recognized that each model had applicability in different portions of the realtime systems industry. Therefore an underlying scheduling mechanism is provided for use by realtime Java threads, but the exact nature of possible scheduling mechanisms is not specified in advance. Thus, a basic scheduler is provided which is priority-based, preemptive, and allows at least 28 unique priorities.

The scheduler employs fixed priorities; the system may not change thread priority, except when required to execute the priority inversion avoidance algorithm (see Section 4.2.3). A thread, however, can change its own priority, or another thread's priority.

Realtime threads for Java

In order to implement realtime scheduling, the realtime Java specification defines a number of *schedulable* objects. Any instance of any class implementing the *Schedulable* interface is a schedulable object, and its scheduling will be managed by the instances of **Scheduler** to which it holds a reference. The three schedulable classes defined by the realtime Java specification are the **RealtimeThread**, the **NoHeapRealtimeThread**, and the **AsyncEventHandler**. The **RealtimeThread** object extends the **java.lang.Thread** object found in the standard Java API, but allows specification of realtime and memory parameters. The **NoHeapRealtimeThread** class allows time-critical threads to execute at a higher priority than the garbage collector. Since an instance of a **NoHeapRealtimeThread** object may immediately preempt the garbage collection function, logic contained in its `run()` method is not allowed to allocate or reference any object allocated in the heap. In conventional Java, the "heap" is the area in the system memory where newly created objects are allocated [3]. The **AsyncEventHandler** class contains code that is scheduled in response to the occurrence of an event; its `run()` method acts like a realtime thread.

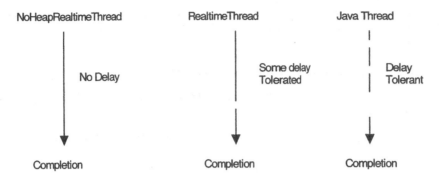

Figure 4.1 *Using Realtime, NoHeapRealtime, and Conventional Java threads.*

NoHeapRealtimeThreads are intended for use by applications which do not tolerate non-scheduled delays. For realtime applications that are more delay-tolerant, **RealtimeThread**s may be employed. Figure 4.1 illustrates the use of the different thread types.

The basic issue involved in design of a realtime system is determining whether or not a given program will complete execution within a given time constraint. This can be determined by program analysis, by testing, or by some combination of both. Implementation of realtime timing constraints is generally accomplished by prioritization of execution threads. A *dispatching* function is used to select the thread for execution which currently has the highest priority. While assignment of priority is under the control of the programmer, the base scheduler also inherits methods from its superclass that permit feasibility analysis (assuming rate monotonic priority assignment).

Parameter classes for realtime threads

A number of parameter classes may be associated with each of the schedulable objects. Each parameter class holds a resource demand characteristic for the schedulable object(s) with which it is associated. For example, a **RealtimeThread** object may have a **SchedulingParameters** class and a **ReleaseParameters** class associated with it. The **SchedulingParameters** class contains a priority value that determines execution eligibility; when a **SchedulingParameters** class is bound to a **RealtimeThread** object, the **RealtimeThread** object takes on the priority assigned by the priority value of the **SchedulingParameters** class. The **ReleaseParameters** class contains parameters related to release of resources, such as relative cost and execution deadline. Methods are provided to enable the values of the parameters to be set and accessed, for example `getSchedulingPara meters()` and `setSchedulingParameters()`.

The default scheduling algorithm is fixed-priority preemptive with at least 28 unique priority levels. The **PriorityScheduler** subclass of **Scheduler** uses this algorithm. However, implementers may wish to develop other scheduling and feasibility analysis algorithms for specific applications.

Code examples for realtime threads

The simplest realtime thread is instantiated by simply creating an instance of **RealtimeThread**:

```
RealtimeThread rtt = new RealtimeThread()
public void run() {
  //body of run() method
}
```

This will create a realtime thread with all parameter values (scheduling parameters, release parameters, etc.) set to null. The default values for null parameter values depend on the value of the default **Scheduler** at the time the thread is created. To create a realtime thread with scheduling parameters, a **SchedulingParameters** object must be created which specifies the relative or absolute priority of the thread:

```
//relative priority
SchedulingParameters sp =
new PriorityParameters
  (PriorityScheduler.getMaxPriority());
RealtimeThread rtt = new RealtimeThread(sp)
public void run() {
  //body of run() method
}
//absolute priority
SchedulingParameters sp =
new PriorityParameters(int priority);
RealtimeThread rtt = new RealtimeThread(sp)
public void run() {
  //body of run() method
}
```

A **NoHeapRealtimeThread** must specify a **ScopedMemory** or **ImmortalMemory** area for execution:

```
MemoryArea ma =
new ImmortalMemory.instance();
NoHeapRealtimeThread nrt =
  new NoHeapRealtimeThread(sp, ma)
public void run() {
  //body of run() method - may not
  //reference objects in heap
}
```

4.2.2 Memory management

In realtime applications, it is important for memory resources to be available when new objects are created. Also, garbage collection should not cause long delays at unpredictable times. The standard version of Java implements garbage collection as a low-priority background thread; this can cause problems in CPU-intensive applications where the garbage collection function might not be invoked until the system runs out of memory resources. The realtime Java experts group sought to define a memory allocation and reclamation specification that would

- Be independent of any particular garbage collection algorithm;
- Allow the program to precisely characterize an implemented garbage collection algorithm's effect on the execution time, preemption, and dispatching of realtime Java threads;
- Allow the allocation and reclamation of objects outside of any interference by a garbage collection algorithm.

Memory areas

While the standard version of Java uses the concept of the "heap" for memory allocation for all objects, the realtime Java specification provides four distinct types of memory allocation and management by defining four separate memory "areas." The areas defined in the specification are:

- *Scoped memory*. Scoped memory is used to allocate memory for classes of objects that have a lifetime defined by syntactic scope.
- *Physical memory*. Physical memory allows objects to be created within specific physical memory regions that have specific characteristics, such as memory that has substantially faster access.
- *Immortal memory*. Immortal memory represents an area of memory containing objects that exist from the time they are allocated until the application is terminated.
- *Heap memory*. Management of heap memory is identical to that employed in the standard Java implementation. The realtime Java specification does not affect the lifetime of objects on the heap.

The **MemoryArea** abstract class is the base class of all classes dealing with allocatable memory areas. **HeapMemory**, **ImmortalMemory**, **ImmortalPhysicalMemory**, and **ScopedMemory** are all subclasses of **MemoryArea**. Figure 4.2 illustrates the different memory areas and their characteristics. The **HeapMemory** class is a singleton object that allows logic within other scoped memory to allocate objects in the Java heap. **ImmortalMemory** objects are not subject to garbage collection, and exist until the application termi-

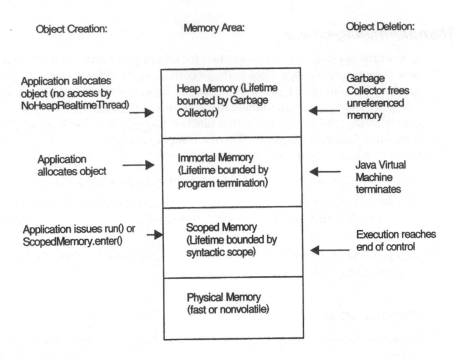

Figure 4.2 *Realtime Java memory areas and characteristics.*

nates. The **ImmortalPhysicalMemory** class allows objects to be allocated from a range of physical memory with particular attributes determined by their memory type. **ScopedMemory** is defined and discussed below.

Scoped memory

A *memory scope* is used to define limits on the lifetime of objects allocated within it. Within it, every use of new (i.e. every creation of a new instance) causes the memory to be allocated from the active memory scope. A scope may be defined explicitly, or it may be specified as an attribute of a **RealtimeThread**. A scope is explicitly defined by using the enter() method of a **MemoryArea** object; it may also be defined by specifying a **ScopedMemory** area object as a parameter of a **RealtimeThread** (or **NoHeapRealtimeThread**).

Every scoped memory area maintains a count of external references to that memory area. The count is increased every time an enter() method for that **MemoryArea** is executed, or by the creation of a **RealtimeThread** using the specified **ScopedMemory** area object. The count is decreased when the enter() method returns, or when the **RealtimeThread** using the **ScopedMemory** object exits. When the count drops to zero, the finalize method for each object in the memory is executed to completion. The scope cannot be reused until finalization is complete.

Scopes may be nested. When a nested scope is entered, memory is allocated from the area associated with the new scope. When the nested scope is exited, memory is again allocated from the area associated with the previous scope.

Because the lifetime of each scoped memory area is unique, there are restrictions relating to the use of references to scoped memory area objects:

1. A reference to an object in **ScopedMemory** can never be stored in an object allocated in the Java heap.

2. A reference to an object in **ScopedMemory** can never be stored in an object allocated in **ImmortalMemory**.

3. A reference to an object in **ScopedMemory** can only be stored in objects allocated in the same **ScopedMemory** area, or into a (more inner) **ScopedMemory** area nested by the use of its enter() method.

4. References to immortal or heap objects may be stored in an object allocated in a **ScopedMemory** area.

The virtual machine must be capable of detecting illegal assignment attempts and throwing an appropriate exception when they occur.

4.2.3 Synchronization and resource sharing

In the standard Java platform, the *synchronized* keyword is used to protect critical sections of code from simultaneous access by multiple tasks. No other task may access protected code until the current task has exited. This implementation of synchronization may make it difficult for realtime programmers to estimate the amount of time that a given task will have to wait to gain access to synchronized code. Also, a technique for dealing with priority inversion must be specified. Priority inversion occurs when a thread attempts to acquire a lock that is held by a lower-priority thread; the priority of the lower-priority thread is, in effect, raised to the priority of the higher-priority thread during the interval that the lower-priority thread holds the lock. The realtime Java implementation must provide an algorithm for avoidance of priority inversion as part of its implementation of monitors. In addition, it must provide wait-free queue classes, both to prevent priority inversion and to allow a thread to have an execution priority higher than that of the garbage collection.

For both the processor and synchronized blocks, threads waiting to acquire a resource must be released in execution eligibility order. If threads have the same execution eligibility under the active scheduling policy, such threads are awakened in FIFO order. Rules for wait queues are as follows:

- Threads waiting to enter synchronized blocks are granted access to the synchronized block in execution eligibility order.

- A blocked thread that becomes ready to run is given access to the processor in execution eligibility order.

- A thread whose execution eligibility is explicitly set by itself or another thread is given access to the processor in execution eligibility order.

- A thread that performs a yield will be given access to the processor after waiting threads of the same execution eligibility.

- Threads that are preempted in favor of a thread with higher execution eligibility may be given access to the processor at any time as determined by a particular implementation. The implementation is required to provide documentation stating exactly the algorithm used for granting such access.

Priority inversion avoidance

All implementations must provide monitors using the synchronized primitive that ensure that there is no unbounded priority inversion; this must apply to code run within the implementation as well as realtime threads. The priority inheritance protocol must be implemented by default [4]. The realtime Java specification also allows the default policy to be overridden for a particular monitor, provided that the policy is supported by the implementation.

Priority ceiling emulation protocol (highest locker protocol) is also specified for systems that support it. In this policy, a monitor is created with a *priority ceiling* that specifies the highest priority of any thread that could attempt to enter it. As soon as a thread enters synchronized code, its priority is raised to the monitor's ceiling priority. This ensures mutually exclusive access to the code, since it will not be preempted by any thread that could possibly attempt to enter the same monitor. If a thread has a higher priority than the priority ceiling of the monitor it is attempting to enter (presumably through programming error), an exception is thrown.

As the realtime Java specification points out, it is not possible for **NoHeapRealtimeThreads** and regular Java threads to synchronize on the same object and still avoid priority inversion, given the rules stated above. Since **NoHeapRealtimeThreads** always have an execution eligibility priority higher than that of the garbage collector, and regular Java threads never have an execution eligibility priority higher than that of the garbage collector, no known priority inversion avoidance algorithm can be used, since the algorithm may not raise the priority of the regular Java thread higher than that of the garbage collector.

Wait-free queue classes

To provide protected, non-blocking, shared access by both **NoHeapRealtimeThreads** and regular Java threads to objects, the realtime Java specification provides three wait-free queue classes: **WaitFreeDequeue**;

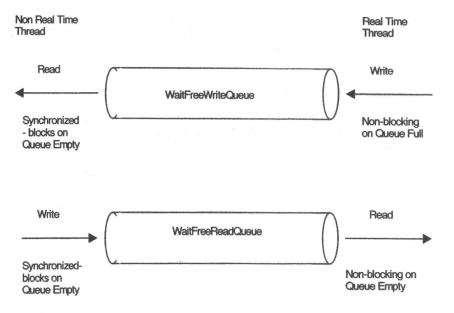

Figure 4.3   *Use of WaitFreeWriteQueue and WaitFreeReadQueue classes*

WaitFreeReadQueue; and **WaitFreeWriteQueue**. The **WaitFreeWriteQueue** class allows a realtime thread to write unidirectionally to a non-realtime thread without incurring delay due to blocking by the non-realtime thread; conversely, the **WaitFreeReadQueue** allows a realtime thread to read from a non-realtime thread without delay due to blocking by the non-realtime thread. If the memory areas for the realtime and non-realtime threads are different, the queue will use the more restrictive of the two. Figure 4.3 illustrates the use of the **WaitFreeWriteQueue** and the **WaitFreeReadQueue**.

4.2.4 Asynchronous event handling

Since events in the real world occur asynchronously with respect to realtime systems, an efficient means of handling asynchronous events must be provided. Classes for specific events are provided as part of the realtime Java specification, and a scheduler is provided to schedule and dispatch the event handling logic.

Two classes are provided to support asynchronous event handling. An **AsyncEvent** object represents something that happens in the real world which is of interest to the realtime system, such as a POSIX signal or a hardware interrupt. When such an event occurs, a `handleAsyncEvent()` method of an instance of **AsyncEventHandler** is scheduled and performs the operation required by the event. An instance of **AsyncEvent** manages the set of handlers associated with the event, and the unblocking of handlers when the event is fired. An instance of **AsyncEventHandler** is similar to a thread; it is a schedulable class as well as being a runnable object. It has instances of **ReleaseParameters**, **SchedulingParameters**, and **MemoryParameters** associated with it that control the execution of the handler once the associated **AsyncEvent** is fired.

Example code for asynchronous event handling

Asynchronous event handling for realtime Java makes use of the standard Java event handling mechanism by enabling event handlers to be associated with user-specified events:

```
AsyncEventHandler ioh = new AsyncEventHandler() {
  public void handleAsyncEvent() {
    //perform some action based on event occurrence
  }
};

AsyncEvent ae = new AsyncEvent();
ae.addHandler(ioh);
```

However, since asynchronous events, like threads, are schedulable in realtime Java, it is possible to specify their execution priority. To set high (maximum) priority for a handler, the following could be employed:

```
SchedulingParameters sph =
new PriorityParameters
  (PriorityScheduler.getMaxPriority());
AsyncEventHandler ioh1 =
  new AsyncEventHandler(sph, null, null, null, null) {
  public void handleAsyncEvent() {
    //perform some action based on event occurrence
  }
};
```

A **POSIXSignalHandler** class is provided to enable use of asynchronous event handlers to perform operations triggered by POSIX signals from the underlying operating systems. To associate the high-priority event handler described above with the occurrence of a POSIX SIGIO (socket I/O possible) event, the following could be used:

```
POSIXSignalHandler.addHandler(SIGIO, ioh1);
```

Timers

Two specialized types of **AsyncEvent** are the **OneShotTimer** and the **PeriodicTimer**; as their names suggest, the **OneShotTimer** fires once at a specified time, while the **PeriodicTimer** fires periodically at a specified interval. Timers are driven by **Clock** objects. A special **Clock** object, `Clock.getRealtime Clock()`, represents the realtime clock.

4.2.5 Asynchronous transfer of control

The realtime Java specification allows for the transfer of execution from one location in the software to another in an asynchronous manner. This capability extends the standard Java exception handling mechanism to permit transfer of control in another Java thread (within applications that permit asynchronous transfer of control).

In iterative algorithms where the computational cost is highly variable, and successive iterations produce increasingly refined results, it may be desirable to determine a time bound on how long to execute the computation before beginning an asynchronously transfer control to the result reporting function when the time limit is met.

Individual threads must specify whether or not asynchronous transfer of control is allowed. For threads which allow it, there may be sections of code which must be allowed to execute to completion. These sections are indicated by means of synchronized methods and statements.

Asynchronous transfer of control can be triggered in a target thread either directly from a source thread, or indirectly by means of an asynchronous event handler. Asynchronous transfer of control may be triggered by any asynchronous event, including a timer firing.

4.2.6 Asynchronous thread termination

It is convenient to provide a means for terminating execution of a thread, based on changes in the external system. Earlier versions of Java provided `stop()` and `destroy()` methods for this purpose; however, `stop()` could leave shared objects in an inconsistent state, and `destroy()` could result in a deadlock if it is invoked while the thread is holding a lock. The realtime Java specification provides asynchronous thread termination through the use of asynchronous event handling and asynchronous transfer of control. Asynchronous event handlers can be created to react to external events; on detection of specified events, they can invoke the `interrupt()` method on the affected thread. The `interrupt()` method sets the state of the **AsynchronouslyInterruptedException** to pending. Interruptible methods may then transfer control to appropriate catch clauses.

4.2.7 Physical memory access

Many realtime applications require direct access and manipulation of physical memory. The realtime Java specification defines classes which permit byte-level access to physical memory and allow the construction of objects in physical memory. A **PhysicalMemoryFactory** must be implemented to create instances of physical memory objects; `create()` methods in the individual physical memory classes are used to create instances of the required physical memory object using the factory. The **RawMemoryAccess** class allows creation of an object which represents a range of physical addresses, and provides get/set access at byte, short, int, long, float, and double granularity. A **RawMemoryAccess** object may not contain objects or references to objects, as this would defeat type-checking. Byte ordering interpretation (e.g. big-endian or little-endian) is set by the BYTE_ORDER static variable in class **RealtimeSystem**. The **RawMemoryAccess** class allows a realtime program to implement low-level memory-resident functions such as device drivers, memory-mapped I/O, and flash memory.

The **ScopedPhysicalMemory** and **ImmortalPhysicalMemory** classes allow creation of objects which represent a range of physical memory addresses in which Java objects may be located. These classes allow realtime programs to access memory at specific addresses for performance or other reasons (e.g. access to fast static RAM).

4.2.8 Errors and exceptions

A number of new errors and exceptions are defined to support realtime functions. As in standard Java, errors generally signify a non-recoverable condition, while exceptions signify an abnormal condition that must be caught and handled to prevent program termination.

Errors

Errors specific to realtime Java include the **MemoryAccessError**, which is thrown by the Java virtual machine when a thread attempts to access memory that is not in scope. A **ThrowBoundaryError** occurs when a throwable tries to propagate into a scope where it is not accessible. An **IllegalAssignmentError** is thrown on an attempt to make an illegal assignment. A **ResourceLimitError** is thrown if an attempt is made to exceed a system resource limit, such as the maximum number of locks. Table 4.1 lists new errors defined in the realtime Java specification.

Exceptions

New exception classes defined for realtime Java include the **Asynchronously InterruptedException**, which is generated when a thread is asynchronously interrupted. (More information on the **AsynchronouslyInterruptedException** is given below.) The **MemoryScopeException** is thrown by the write methods of the **Wait FreeDequeue**, **WaitFreeReadQueue**, and **WaitFreeWriteQueue** classes if the ends of the queues are in incompatible memory areas. The **OffsetOutOfBounds**

Table 4.1 Errors for realtime Java

Error	Definition	Thrown by
MemoryAccessError	Thrown by the JVM when a thread attempts to access memory that is not in scope	Thrown on an attempt to refer to an object in an inaccessible **MemoryArea**. For example, **MemoryAccessError** will be thrown if logic in a **NoHeapRealtimeThread** attempts to refer to an object in the Java heap.
ThrowBoundaryError	A throwable tried to propagate into a scope where it was not accessible	`enter()` method
IllegalAssignmentError	Thrown on an attempt to make an illegal assignment	For Example, will be thrown if logic attempts to assign a reference to an object in **ScopedMemory** to a field in an object in **ImmortalMemory**
ResourceLimitError	Thrown if an attempt is made to exceed a system resource limit, such as the maximum number of locks	`SetMaximumConcurrentLocks()` method of RealtimeSystem

Exception is generated by the physical memory classes when the given offset is out of bounds. The **SizeOutOfBoundsException** is generated by the physical memory classes when the given size is out of bounds. The **UnsupportedPhysicalMemory Exception** is generated by the physical memory classes when the requested physical memory is unsupported.

The **AsynchronouslyInterruptedException** plays a major role in the implementation of asynchronous transfer of control. Including an **Asynchronously InterruptedException** in the throws clause of a method indicates its ability to be asynchronously interrupted at any time. If a thread is interrupted while executing a method with this exception, then an instance of **AsynchronouslyInterrupted Exception** will be executed as soon as the thread is executing a section of code that permits asynchronous interruption (i.e. is outside of any section in which asynchronous transfer of control is deferred).

Instances of `AsynchronouslyInterruptedException` may be generated by either program logic, or by internal virtual machine mechanisms that operate asynchronously to the program logic that is the target of the exception. The realtime Java specification requires that blocking methods in java.io must be prevented from blocking indefinitely when invoked from a method with this exception in its `throws` clause. When either `Asynchronously InterruptedException.fire()` or `RealtimeThread.interrupt()` is called on a java.io method invoked from an interruptible method, the implementation may (1) unblock the blocked call, (2) raise an IOException on behalf of the call, or (3) allow the call to complete normally if the implementation determines that the call would eventually unblock. Program logic within a synchronized block in a method which includes an **AsynchronouslyInterruptedException** cannot receive an instance of this exception; the interrupted state of the execution context is set to pending, and the program logic will receive the instance when execution passes out of the synchronized block.

Table 4.2 lists new exceptions defined in the realtime Java specification.

Table 4.2 Exceptions for realtime Java

Exception	Definition	Thrown By
AsynchronouslyInterruptedException	Generated when a thread is asynchronously interrupted	`interrupt()` method of **RealtimeThread** or **NoHeapRealtimeThread** `interruptAction()` method of **Interruptible**
MemoryScopeException	Thrown by the wait-free queue implementation if construction of any of the wait-free queues is attempted with the ends of the queues in incompatible memory areas	`blockingWrite()` and `nonBlockingWrite()` methods of **WaitFreeDequeue** write() method of WaitFreeWriteQueue
OffsetOutOfBoundsException	Generated by the physical memory classes when the given offset is out of bounds	`create()` method of **ImmortalPhysicalMemory**, **ScopedPhysicalMemory**, **RawMemoryAccess**, **RawMemoryFloatAccess** `get/setByte()`, `get/setBytes()`, `get/setInt()`, `get/setInts()`, `get/setLong()`, `get/setLongs()`, `get/setShort()`, `get/setShorts()`, methods of **RawMemoryAccess** `get/setDouble()`, `get/setDoubles()`, `get/setFloat()`, `getFloats()` methods of **RawMemoryFloatAccess**

Table 4.2 (*continued*)

Exception	Definition	Thrown By
SizeOutOfBoundsException	Generated by the physical memory classes when the given size is out of bounds	`create()` method of **ImmortalPhysicalMemory**, **ScopedPhysicalMemory**, **RawMemoryAccess**, **RawMemoryFloatAccess**
		`get/setByte()`, `get/setBytes()`, `get/setInt()`, `get/setInts()`, `get/setLong()`, `get/setLongs()`, `get/setShort()`, `get/setShorts()`, methods of **RawMemoryAccess**
		`get/setDouble()`, `get/setDoubles()`, `get/setFloat()`, `getFloats()` methods of **RawMemoryFloatAccess**
UnsupportedPhysicalMemoryException	Generated by the physical memory classes when the requested physical memory is unsupported	`create()` method of **ImmortalPhysicalMemory**, **ScopedPhysicalMemory**, **RawMemoryAccess**, **RawMemoryFloatAccess**

References

1. Liu CL, Layland JW. Scheduling algorithms for multiprogramming in a hard-realtime environment. J. ACM 1973;20(1):44–61.
2. Bollella G, Brosgol B, Furr S, Hardin D, Dibble P, Gosling J, Turnbull M, The real-time specification for Java. Boston, MA: Addison-Wesley, 2000. Available online at http://java.sun.com/aboutJava/communityprocess/first/jsr001/index.html.
3. Arnold K, Gosling J. The Java programming language. Reading, MA, Addison-Wesley, 1996, p. 9.
4. The priority inheritance protocol is an algorithm used for realtime scheduling. Briefly, if thread t_1 attempts to acquire a lock that is held by a lower-priority thread t_2, then t_2's priority is raised to that of t_1 as long as t_2 holds the lock (and recursively if t_2 is itself waiting to acquire a lock held by an even lower-priority thread). See, for example, Sha L, Rajkumar R, Lehoczky JP. Priority inheritance protocols: an approach to real-time synchronization. IEEE Trans. Computers 1990;39(9):1175–1185.

5

Java for network management

Anirban Sharma

ONI Systems, Inc., USA

5.1 Introduction

The recent growth of the Internet and the resulting demand for bandwidth has caused the service providers to build out their networks at an incredible pace. As networks grow in size, speed and flexibility, it is important that service providers are able to efficiently provision, monitor and troubleshoot these networks. Network management is an integral component in today's network design. A comprehensive network management solution that is scaleable, reliable and can be distributed, is absolutely required by service providers while evaluating network equipment from vendors for deployment.

However, there are several challenges in designing such a network management system. Often service providers have a hodge-podge of networking gear from multiple vendors in their networks. This complicates the design of any such software as it has to now manage multiple types of network elements. The standards defined for network management are either immature or exceedingly complex adding to this challenge. Moreover, most of the standards have room for proprietary extensions, which each vendor may implement differently. Service providers also require network management software to run on multiple operating systems and hardware platforms. In addition to all these, network management systems must be agile enough to be able to support the ever-changing networking technologies.

In this chapter we explore how to use Sun's Java programming language to develop network management software that can meet these challenges. Java offers a simple and object-oriented programming environment which is portable and architecture neutral. With support for developing enterprise applications that are distributed, transaction-aware and persistent, it makes an ideal choice for developing enterprise applications like network management systems.

5.2 Network management concepts

Before we get into the details of how to use Java in developing network management systems, let's take a moment to review some of the basic concepts that are useful for understanding architectures explained in subsequent sections.

5.2.1 Layers of network management

The functionality for managing a network can be divided into several layers, each with its own specific responsibility [1] (Figure 5.1). They can be described as follows:

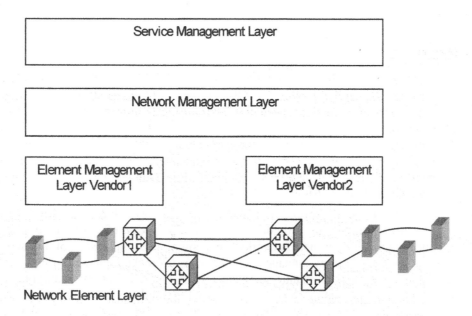

Figure 5.1 *TMN layers for network management.*

- Network element layer (NEL): a network element can be a workstation, router, ATM switch, digital cross connect, add-drop multiplexor or any other network connected device. It is the device that needs to be managed by a network management system. The network element may provide a very limited set of management functionality for initial turn-up and command access through a craft interface.

- Element management layer (EML): the process of configuring, monitoring and controlling any network element can be partitioned into this layer. Management activities include issuing commands to control the flow of the network traffic, configuring parameters such as IP address of the network element, reading counters for statistical measurements.

- Network management layer (NML): element management is responsible for controlling individual network elements whereas network management provides an overall network view and is able to perform operations within or across the complete breadth of the network. Creating end-to-end circuits, testing the integrity of trunks between nodes, defining preferred paths for network traffic flow are some of the responsibilities of a network management application. Typically network management systems are deployed in a network operations center (NOC) which acts as a focal point for performing network-wide operations such as provisioning, monitoring the health of the network and statistical data collection.

- Service management layer (SML): service management deals with the processes required to monitor, command and control the actual services delivered by the network elements. These services can be IP service, frame relay, ATM, ESCON, etc. Associated with these services are features like guaranteed quality of service, service level agreements, usage-based billing, advanced performance monitoring, customer network management, etc. These are value added services above and beyond the basic network transport access. Many service providers use these mechanisms to differentiate themselves from their competitors.

Abstracting out the management responsibility into different layers lets us deal with only a limited set of features at each layer. However, this also raises additional architectural considerations for being distributed and transactional across the management domains.

5.2.2 Functional areas

According to the ITU-T [2,3], network management can be vertically divided into five different functional areas:

- Configuration management: this functional area deals with provisioning of the equipment in the network element, adding, deleting or modifying circuits, configuring multiple network elements in a topology to form a network, etc.

- Fault management: the functionality of monitoring the network elements for any faults, alarms or events can be termed as fault management. In a network management setting, faults from individual network elements gathered by their element management software may be correlated to present a network wide view.

- Accounting management: mechanisms for billing customers for using network resources is supported by the accounting management functional area. This involves accurate book keeping of usage statistics, interfacing with the configuration management functional area to get triggers of when circuits are created and torn down, interfacing with fault management to get information of SLA violations, etc.

- Performance management: this functional area deals with collection of data about the network in order to derive usage statistics, load information, etc. in order to efficiently plan for expansion of the network or monitor for patterns in the network that may need increased attention for failures.

- Security management: maintaining integrity of the network while managing it efficiently is of paramount importance to service providers. Security management deals with issues such as user permissions, user access audits, password authentication, etc. It ensures that the network is secure such that unwanted elements cannot gain access through the management systems.

Partitioning a network management system based on such functional areas can form the basis of the subsystems or packages in the design of the network management system.

5.2.3 Protocols

Protocols used for management of network elements can vary from vendor to vendor. Most of the data communication equipment vendors support simple network management protocol (SNMP) [4] to manage their devices whereas traditional telecommunications equipment vendors use transaction language 1 (TL1) [5]. There are other vendors that use CMIP [6], CORBA [7], XML over HTTP or a proprietary protocol [8]. Since there can be so many different protocols that a network management system has to deal with, it is important that the protocol specific logic is abstracted out so that they can be dealt at an interface level.

5.3 Client–server architectures for network management

In the next few paragraphs we will talk about the evolution of architectures for network management systems. As with any enterprise applications, network management systems have evolved over the years from a traditional two-tier client–server model to an *n*-tier model supporting multiple interfaces.

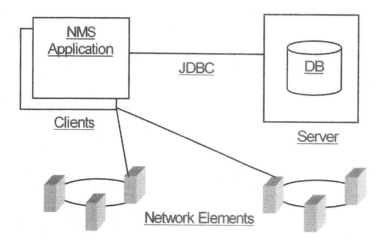

Figure 5.2 *Two-tier NMS architecture.*

In a two-tier model a monolithic application containing the presentation and the business logic in the client tier would access data from a persistent store (database) in the server tier (Figure 5.2). The client tier would make protocol specific calls to the network elements to send commands and receive messages from autonomous events occurring in the element. It would update the database as a result of these asynchronous events. This architecture is not very scaleable. As changes are made to the network elements as part of enhancements or new features, the network management application has to be constantly updated as there is such a tight coupling between the two. A traditional two-tier implementation can be realized with a swing application containing all the business logic, accessing the database using JDBC. Since most of the logic is implemented in the client tier, clients must run on machines that have enough horsepower to support such applications. Thus, performance of the application becomes dependent on the processing power of the client. This increases capital expenditure spending for service providers when deploying such software in a NOC setting where each operator requiring access to manage the network needs to have a powerful workstation that can run the heavyweight network management application.

As an improvement from the traditional two-tier model, network management systems evolved into a three-tier approach (Figure 5.3). Here, presentation logic was separated from the business logic. The client tier was limited only to presentation related functionality, and became the so-called "thin client." For any business logic rules or validation, the client would make a call to the server. The business logic in the server which forms the second tier could now be shared among multiple clients. In a distributed setting, the server could be deployed in a enterprise class machine with enough processing power, memory and other resources, where as the clients could be deployed in cheaper machines sufficient enough to run only the presentation logic. Besides all the common functionality for making the manage-

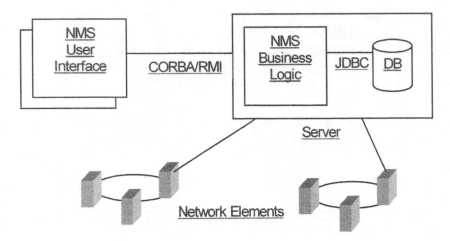

Figure 5.3 *Three-tier NMS architecture.*

ment software transaction-aware, persistent security can now be implemented in one place – the server. The business logic also encapsulates the functionality of sending commands to the network element and receiving events from it. In the third tier of a three-tier model, we still have the database which can be accessed only through the business logic in the second tier. A three-tier implementation can have a swing application in the client tier accessing a server using a distributed transport mechanism like RMI or CORBA. The server uses JDBC to access the database and may have adapters for handling native management protocols like TL1 and SNMP.

Using the three-tier approach, more scaleable network management applications can now be developed. The network management system can be distributed where hundreds of clients can now access the server to manage the network. As more users needs to be supported, only the server machine needs to be upgraded. This solution provides greater manageability and cost-effectiveness for the service providers.

With the advent of the Web, as more and more enterprise applications are using a web browser as the universal user interface, service providers are requiring network management systems to be web enabled. For a web-based system we use an *n*-tier model where the web browser is in the client tier, the web server and the business logic form the middle tiers and the database makes the fourth tier (Figure 5.4). Such a solution can be deployed on thin clients requiring the machines in the client tier with just enough processing power to run a web browser. The number of users that can be supported for managing a network based on such architecture is huge. Moreover, with a web-based network management system, service providers can get their operators to manage the network from any machine that can run a web browser. This greatly improves accessibility of the management system, however there are now additional issues like security to deal with. An *n*-tier network management system can be realized by using a J2EE compliant application server in the middle tiers. An application server includes a web server and support for

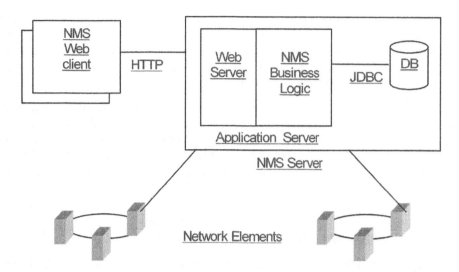

Figure 5.4 *n-Tier architecture of a network management system.*

enterprise Java APIs like Java server pages (JSPs), servlets and enterprise Java Beans (EJBs).

5.4 J2EE and application servers

The Java 2 Platform, Enterprise Edition (J2EE) [9] defines the standard for developing *n*-tier enterprise applications. J2EE provides the infrastructure APIs that are needed to rapidly deploy scalable applications. These include standards for server side business components using EJBs [10], transactions using Java transaction service (JTS) [11], messaging using Java message service (JMS) [12], naming and directory services using Java naming and directory interface (JNDI) [13], dynamic web page generation using servlets and JSPs [14].

J2EE provides the basic plumbing for developing multi-tier applications. Time-to-market of a scalable network management solution is crucial for telecommunications equipment vendors today. Building them on top of standardized interfaces can significantly reduce the design-build-deploy cycle and at the same time promote interoperability between such applications. The developers can focus on the business logic of the product rather then spending time and resources on system or middleware issues.

5.4.1 Enterprise Java Beans (EJBs)

EJBs is Sun's standard for developing server side Java components. Using the container–component architecture, EJBs lets developers easily build business logic components with the container providing the infrastructure for services like look-up, persistence, transaction, security, etc. There is a well defined contract between the component and the container. The specification defines the use of deployment descriptors for EJBs which lets deployers of these components tune and specify properties at runtime without any code change.

The EJB specification defines two types of component: session beans and entity beans. Session beans are generally transient and implement the business methods of an application. Entity beans have state and map well to the persistent storage. EJBs may leverage other enterprise Java APIs like JMS for messaging, JDBC for database access, JNDI for look-ups, etc. to rapidly build enterprise business applications.

5.4.2 Java server pages (JSPs)and servlets

JSPs is a standard for generating dynamic web pages on the server side. JSP lets the web developer embed Java code within HTML. The web server on getting a request for a JSP parses these JSP tags, compiles them, executes them and substitutes their result into the output stream before sending it back to the browser. This enables HTML designers to come up with the layout of the web pages and then have Java developers plug-in the Java code for the dynamic content in the page. JSPs are converted to servlets which are Java classes with HTML adaptation capabilities. JSPs are compiled the first time the request comes in. For subsequent times, the compiled class is used to service HTTP requests. If the JSP gets changed, the class loader of the web server detects it and recompiles before serving it again. JSPs provide a very fast and easy way to deploy web-based applications where a lot of the content served is dynamic, based on the request parameters.

5.4.3 Java Message Service (JMS)

JMS defines a set of standard interfaces to implement messaging in enterprise applications. It can work in conjunction with other enterprise Java APIs like EJB, JTS to provide a powerful infrastructure for building distributed applications. A JMS application either uses the point-to-point (PTP) or publish-and-subscribe (pub/sub) style of messaging. PTP messaging is built around the concept of message queues. Each message is addressed to a specific queue: clients extract messages from the queues established to hold their messages. On the other hand, pub/sub clients address messages to some node in a content hierarchy. Publishers and subscribers are generally anonymous and may dynamically publish or subscribe to the content hierarchy. The system takes care of distributing the messages arriving from a node's multiple publishers to its multiple subscribers. JMS provides client interfaces tailored for each domain.

5.4.4 Application servers

In the last few years a new breed of middleware has emerged that provides all the basic infrastructure required to rapidly deploy enterprise applications. This middleware known as application servers includes a web server and support for enterprise APIs like EJB, JMS, JSP, servlets, JNDI, etc. Since they are geared more towards Internet applications with thousands of simultaneous users, these application servers have features like thread pooling, database connection pooling, object life-cycle management, caching, etc. that are meant to improve scalability and performance. An application server may be used to quickly deploy an n-tier network management system. The application servers usually come with tools that can be used to monitor them (threads, db connections, users, etc.) during deployment.

Service providers often require that these application servers be deployed in a clustered environment for fail over in 24/7 operations with four nines of reliability (99.99% uptime). The software needs to be able to recover from any hardware or network failure with losing visibility of the managed network elements. It is important to consider any such requirements before deciding on your application server platform. There are several J2EE compliant application servers in the market today including the ones from BEA Systems (Weblogic) [15], IBM (Websphere) [16] and iPlanet [17].

5.5 Design considerations

In this section we will consider an n-tier architecture for a network management system based on the concepts that we have learnt so far (Figure 5.5). We will use J2EE as the basis for this architecture. Before getting into the details of the architecture, let us first consider a few requirements for this network management system. The requirements can be annotated as follows:

1. The network management system must be scaleable and distributed. This means that as the number of users grow, more computing resources can be added to support the new load. The system will be distributed in that some functions may be performed in more than one machine.

2. The network management system must support all the management functional areas including fault, configuration, accounting, performance and security management.

3. The network management system must encapsulate all the details about the network elements and their management protocol such that future support for new network elements and management protocols can be added incrementally.

4. The network management system must be able to interoperate with other management systems.

5. The network management system must be able to support traditional GUIs in a

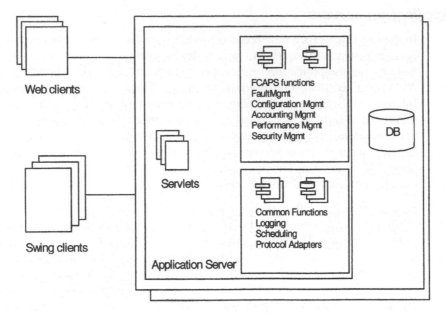

Figure 5.5 *Functional architecture of the network management system.*

NOC setting and also support web-based access for customer network management and greater accessibility.

So based on the above requirements we make the following design decisions:

- The network management system will be based on an *n*-tier architecture. An application server will be used for the middle tiers. The application server must have support for clustering.

- The business logic of the network management system will be implemented using EJBs. User operations will be mapped to session EJBs. Entity beans will be used to manage persistence store of the managed objects. Management functional areas will be implemented as a collection of session and entity beans.

- Common network management functions such as logging, scheduling, back-up, administration, etc. will also be implemented as session and entity beans.

- The network management system will encapsulate native management protocols into adapters. As support for new types of network elements with a different management protocols are added, a new protocol adapter should be pluggable into the framework of the system.

5.5.1 Presentation logic

The web browser has become a universal user interface today. Users are already familiar with it in their day-to-day life. Being able to manage a network using a web browser as an interface has significant advantages. The users can manage their network from any workstation that has a browser installed. The client machines need to be powerful enough to run a web browser. The web-based GUI is implemented using JSP and servlets. In JSP development, the format of the web page can be first laid out using popular HTML editing tools. JSP tags are used to write Java code in portions of the page where dynamic data is needed from the server. In the case of servlets, a Java class is written to generate the same HTML output. All the business logic for the network management application including JSPs and servlets resides in the server side.

However, one of the drawbacks of using a browser-based interface is the poor usability and responsiveness of the system. When an alarm occurs in a network element, the user may expect to see a pop-up screen or some other visual indication autonomously. This is awkward to implement in a web-based client which works on a request–response paradigm. So, to offer a better GUI experience to the user, a swing-based client can be provided. Using swing controls, usability and responsiveness of the GUI can be significantly improved. Data can be cached in the GUI while working through a series of screens rather then sending and fetching it each time from the server as is the case with a browser-based client.

In either case, the presentation layer makes invocations on the session EJBs to perform various user operations.

5.5.2 Business logic

This consists of session EJBs and entity EJBs. Session EJBs implement the actual business logic of the application. A typical network management application may have session beans to implement fault, configuration, accounting, performance and security management functional areas. Session beans validate the input data, send commands to the network element, update the NMS persistent storage and publish asynchronous messages for interested subscribers.

Session beans may call other session beans (e.g. a configuration session bean to set up virtual circuits may call methods on another session bean that creates the termination points). A session bean may also invoke methods on an entity bean to leverage the data from a data store. Entity beans encapsulate the data tier of an *n*-tier application. Entity beans typically map to a row of a table in a relational database. They can also work with object databases using the containers that the object database vendors provide, to work with a J2EE compliant application server.

Both session and entity beans have transactional attributes. They can be declared in their deployment descriptor to participate in a transaction. When a client of the session bean makes a call on the session bean, the container transparently starts a transaction. All the EJBs that are being used in a call may participate in the same transaction. If all the operations return successfully without any exceptions, the transaction is committed, otherwise the transaction is rolled back by the container.

EJB containers use the JTS API to provide this functionality. It is worth noting here that the application developer does not have to code anything in the EJBs to provide such transactional features, they are built into the infrastructure of the application server. Built-in transaction support is crucial for rapidly deploying enterprise applications like network management systems.

The business logic of the network management system can be partitioned into two categories – common functions and FCAPS functions. Provisioning, alarm monitoring, performance data collection, authorization and authentication, etc. make up the FCAPS functions. Components that provide functionality such as logging, scheduling, backup, restore, protocol adaptation can be grouped under common functions. These are horizontal features of the system that may be used by one or more of the FCAPS functions. EJBs can be implemented to support both these categories.

The session beans send commands to the individual network elements using a protocol adapter. The protocol adapter translates Java calls to the native management protocol primitives (TL1, SNMP, CMIP, etc.) and vice-versa. It maps the Java data types to the protocol specific types. It provides a set of APIs for other session beans to use so that the business logic implementation can be isolated from the nuances of the management protocol. This creates a healthy decoupling between the application domain and the transport domain of the network management system. Protocol adapters can be implemented as session beans. As new protocols need to be supported a new session bean can be developed and deployed in the existing application server.

Most of the network management operations are driven by user actions. In the structured interaction for a user action, the browser makes an invocation on the servlet. The servlet then calls methods on a session bean that implements this user action. If the user is using a swing GUI, then calls on the session bean are made from this GUI. The session bean encapsulates the business logic. It may call

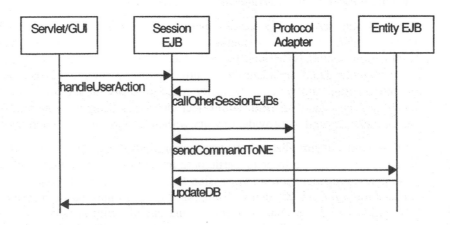

Figure 5.6 *Structured interaction for user actions.*

methods on other session beans and send commands to the network elements. It may then update the persistent store by making calls on the entity beans. Figure 5.6 illustrates interactions for a user action.

5.5.3 Messaging

An important function of network management systems is to monitor for alarms, autonomous messages or SNMP traps from its network elements (Figure 5.7). An event listener can be implemented to listen for all asynchronous messages from the network elements. Internally within the network management system, JMS can be used for messaging between different components. The EJB 2.0 specification defines a new type of bean called MessageDrivenBean. MessageDrivenBeans are used to consume asynchronous JMS messages. In the case of a network management system, such MessageDrivenBeans can be defined for processing alarms, adding log records, handling object creation (OC), object deletion (OD) or attribute-value changes (AVC) from the network elements, processing threshold crossing alerts (TCA), etc.

The event listener can be implemented as a singleton pattern. It will receive all events from the network elements. Once it receives an event, it looks inside it and then publishes a JMS message to a JMS topic that has been previously defined. JMS topics can be defined for alarms, log records, OC, OD, AVC, TCA and others. When a MessageDrivenBean is deployed, it is assigned to handle messages from a specific topic. Any messages sent by a JMS client (in our case the event listener) will be forwarded by the message router to the message bean assigned to receive messages from that topic. When a message is delivered to a message bean, one instance of that bean is selected by the EJB container from a pool to handle the message. The bean instance will receive the message when its onMessage() method is invoked where it can call methods on other session beans. Once the

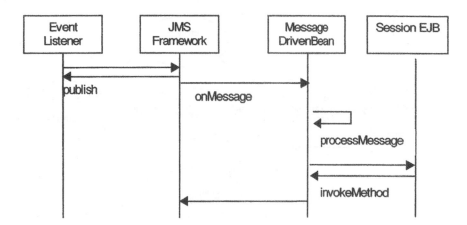

Figure 5.7 *Structured interaction for asynchronous messaging.*

message is consumed, it won't be delivered to any other instance of that message bean, providing that the transaction is not aborted.

Sending asynchronous updates to the GUI client can also be implemented using JMS. GUI objects can register as JMS consumers with interest in specific JMS topics. When a publisher publishes a message on that topic the JMS framework will notify all the registered listeners about it. Asynchronous updates to a browser-based GUI is not feasible unless there is a Java applet running in the browser registered for JMS messages.

Asynchronous handling of messages should be given due diligence during the design so that proper mechanisms can be built into the software to handle the flood of alarms. Most systems fail or behave poorly under scenarios where the network elements are generating a large number of messages within a short interval. A good JMS implementation in an application server should be scaleable to handle the flood of messages. Appropriate throttling mechanisms should be built into the event listener so that it can gracefully handle a large number of messages.

An industrial strength database like Oracle should be used for storing the network management data. The entity EJBs map to tables in the database for storing and retrieving the data in the persistent store. Service providers demand database features like replication for fault tolerance, so it is important to take into account all the database requirements before deciding on one.

5.6 Configuration management example

This example (see Figure 5.8) uses a servlet, a session bean, and a set of entity beans to provide a configuration management query capability for a web-based client. The client first enters a URL for the configuration management application

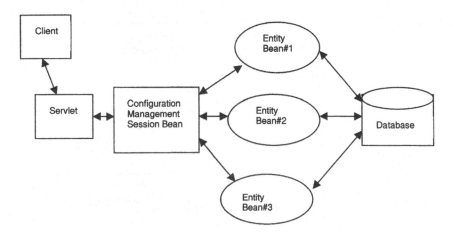

Figure 5.8 *Architectural overview of example configuration management application.*

in his/her browser. The servlet presents the user with a form which requests the user to enter an equipment ID corresponding to an interface unit for which configuration data is desired. (In actual usage, the equipment ID might be a composite identifier consisting of row, frame, shelf and circuit card physical location identifiers.) A session bean is created to process the data input by the user, and to initiate a request for the entity bean corresponding to the equipment ID specified by the user. Each entity bean represents the configuration data associated with a specific equipment ID. For purposes of illustration, the configuration data for each equipment ID consists of the following data items:

- Interface type (e.g. DS1, DS3, OC3, etc.)
- Bandwidth (e.g. 1.544, 44.736, 155 Mb/s)
- Service state (e.g. in-service, out of service)

The data is retrieved from the entity bean and presented to the user via the servlet. (Note that this example does not currently have the ability to create new entity beans representing new equipment ID values; it only allows users to query pre-existing data.)

5.6.1 Functional overview

Servlet functions (request)

1. Client sends request (enters servlet URL).
2. Servlet displays input field and requests entry of equipment ID.
3. Servlet instantiates configuration management session bean.
4. User enters equipment ID and presses submit button.

Session/entity bean functions

1. Session bean references entity bean corresponding to entered equipment ID.
2. Entity bean is loaded with configuration data from database.
3. Session bean retrieves configuration parameters from entity bean.

Servlet functions (response)

1. Servlet displays configuration parameters for the specified equipment ID.

5.6.2 Servlet design

Servlet code

Servlet to display configuration data (ConfigServlet.java)

```java
import java.io.*;
import javax.servlet.*;
import javax.servlet.http.*;
import javax.naming.Context;
import javax.naming.InitialContext;

import Config;
import ConfigHome;

// this servlet provides a simple configuration data query capability.

public class ConfigServlet extends HttpServlet {

  public void init() throws ServletException {

  try {
    // create a JNDI naming context
    InitialContext ic = new InitialContext();
    // retrieve the object bound to the name "Config"
    Object objref = ic.lookup("java:comp/env/ejb/Config'');
    // narrow the reference to a "ConfigHome" object
    ConfigHome home =
      (ConfigHome) PortableRemoteObject.narrow(objref,
        ConfigHome.class);
    // use the "create" method in the home interface to create an
    //instance of Config
    Config equipConfig = home.create();
  } catch (Exception e) {
    e.printStackTrace();
    }
  }

  // when the user clicks the Submit button, the web server
  //calls the doGet method
  public void doGet (HttpServletRequest req,
    HttpServletResponse res)
    throws ServletException, IOException {

    // the servlet fetches the "inputString" parameter
    // corresponding to the Equipment ID
```

```
        // and passes it to the session bean
        String inputString = req.getParameter("inputString");
        // the session bean uses it to request the proper entity bean
        equipConfig.getEquipId(inputString);
        // session bean methods are used to request the configuration
        //parameters
        String IfTyp = equipConfig.getIfTyp(inputString);
        int Bandw = equipConfig.getBandw(inputString);
        String ServState = equipConfig.getServState(inputString);
        // an http response is created of type text/html
        // to display retrieved configuration parameters
        res.setContentType("text/html");
        PrintWriter out = res.getWriter();
        // the generatePage method formats the html page
        // that displays the configuration data
        generatePage(out, IfTyp, Bandw, ServState);
    }

    private void generatePage(PrintWriter out, String IfTyp, int Bandw,
    String ServState) {

      out.println("<html>");
      out.println("<head>");
      out.println("<title>Enter Equipment Identifier to
        Display Configuration Parameters </title>");
      out.println("</head>");
      out.println("<body>");
      out.println("Interface Type = " + IfTyp);
      out.println("<p>");
      out.println("Bandwidth = " + String.valueOf(Bandw));
      out.println("<p>");
      out.println("Service State = " + ServState);
      out.println("<p>");
      out.println("<form method = get action = \"ConfigAlias\">");
      out.println("Please enter an Equipment Identifier: ");
      out.println("<input type = text name = \"inputString\">");
      out.println("<p>");
      out.println("<input type = submit>");
      out.println("</form>");
      out.println("</body>");
      out.println("</html>");
    }
}
```

HTML file (required by the application deployment tool)

config.html

```
<html>
<head>
<title>Initial Page for Configuration Servlet</title>
</head>
<form method = get action = "ConfigAlias">
Please enter an Equipment Identifier
<input type = text name = "inputString">
<p>
<input type = submit>
</form>
</body>
</html>
```

5.6.3 Session bean design

Session beans are intended to last for the duration of a client session. They are not intended to store persistent information. Session beans may be stateless or stateful. Stateful session beans have instance variables which represent the conversational state of the bean. Stateless session beans do not have instance variables; all instances are the same. The Config session bean described below is stateless.

Session bean code

Example Session Bean – Configuration Manager (ConfigEJB.java)

```
import javax.ejb.*;
import javax.naming.Context;
import javax.naming.InitialContext;

public class ConfigEJB implements SessionBean {
  // since the ConfigEJB session bean is stateless, the create method
  //has no arguments
  public void ejbCreate() throws CreateException {}
  // the getEquipId method references the entity bean pointed to by
  //the equipment ID
  public void getEquipId(String inputString) {

    try {
      // create a JNDI naming context
      Context ic = new InitialContext();
```

```
      // retrieve the object bound to the name "Equip"
      Object objref = ic.lookup("java:comp/env/ejb/Equip");
      // narrow the reference to an "EquipHome" object
      EquipHome =
        (EquipHome)PortableRemoteObject.narrow(objref,
          EquipHome.class);
    } catch (Exception re) {
      System.err.println("Couldn't locate Equip Home");
      re.printStackTrace();
      }
    // use the "find by primary key" finder method to find the entity bean
    // corresponding to the specified equipment ID
    String Equip = EquipHome.findByPrimaryKey(inputString);
  }

  // method for returning interface type from entity bean
  public String getIfTyp(String inputString) {
    String Interface = Equip.getInterface();
    return Interface;
  }

  // method for returning bandwidth from entity bean
  public int getBandw(String inputString) {
    int bandwidth = Equip.getBandwidth();
    return bandwidth;
  }
  // method for returning service state from entity bean
  public String getServState(String inputString) {
    String ServiceState = Equip.getServiceState();
    return ServiceState;
  }

  // the following methods are not used, but must be implemented
  public ConfigEJB() {}
  public void ejbRemove() {}
  public void ejbActivate() {}
  public void ejbPassivate() {}
  public void setSessionContext(SessionContext sc) {}

}
```

Home interface

The purpose of the home interface is to define the create methods that a client may invoke. The following code provides a home interface for the Config Session Bean.

```
import java.io.Serializable;
import java.rmi.RemoteException;
import javax.ejb.CreateException;
import javax.ejb.EJBHome;

public interface ConfigHome extends EJBHome {
  Config create() throws RemoteException, CreateException;
}
```

Remote interface

The remote interface defines the business methods that a client may invoke. The remote interface for the Config Session Bean is given below.

```
import java.ejb.EJBObject;
import java.rmi.RemoteException;

public interface Config extends EJBObject {

  public void getEquipId(String inputString) throws RemoteException;
  public String getIfTyp(String inputString) throws RemoteException;
  public int getBandw(String inputString) throws RemoteException;
  public String getServState(String inputString) throws RemoteException;
}
```

5.6.4 Entity bean design

An entity bean represents data kept in a persistent storage mechanism such as a database. For the configuration management example application, entity beans are used to store configuration data for equipment entities. The equipment identifier for each individual device is used as the primary key for identifying the entity bean which contains the configuration data for the device.

Persistence for entity beans may be bean-managed or container-managed. For bean-managed persistence, the code must include the SQL routines that add, store, retrieve, and delete the data to/from the database. For container-managed persistence, the container performs the database functions at the appropriate times. Examples of entity beans for the configuration management example using both bean-managed and container-managed persistence are shown below.

Entity bean code (bean-managed persistence)

Example Entity Bean - Configuration Manager (EquipEJB.java)

```java
import javax.ejb.*;

public class EquipEJB implements EntityBean {

  // the EJB create method for a bean-managed persistence
  // Entity Bean returns a primary key string
  public String ejbCreate(String id, String Interface, int Bandwidth,
    String ServiceState)
    throws CreateException {

    try {
      // the insertRow method includes an SQL insert statement
      insertRow(id, Interface, Bandwidth, ServiceState);
    } catch (Exception ex) {
      throw new EJBException("ejbCreate: " + ex.getMessage());
      }
    this.id = id;
    this.Interface = interface;
    this.Bandwidth = Bandwidth;
    this.ServiceState = ServiceState;

    return id;
  }


  // ejbPostCreate method must be included for each ejbCreate method
  public void ejbPostCreate(String id, String Interface,
    int Bandwidth, String ServiceState)
    throws CreateException {}

  // empty constructor
  public EquipEJB() {}

  // deletes entity bean
  public void ejbRemove() {

    try {
      // deleteRow method includes SQL delete statement
      deleteRow(id);
    } catch (Exception ex) {
      throw new EJBException("ejbremove: " + ex.getMessage());
      }
```

```java
}

// loads current parameters from data base to bean
public void ejbLoad() {

  try {
    loadRow();
  } catch (Exception ex) {
    throw new EJBException("ejbload: " + ex.getMessage());
    }
}

// stores current bean parameter values to data base
public void ejbStore() {

  try {
    storeRow();
  } catch (Exception ex) {
    throw new EJBException("ejbstore: " + ex.getMessage());
    }
}

// allows entity bean search by primary key
public String ejbFindByPrimaryKey(String primaryKey) throws
  FinderException {

  boolean result;

  try {
    result = selectByPrimaryKey(primaryKey);
  } catch (Exception ex) {
    throw new EJBException("ejbFindByPrimaryKey: "
      + ex.getMessage());
    }

  if (result) {
    return primaryKey;
  }
  else {
    throw new ObjectNotFoundException
      ("Row for id " + primaryKey + " not found.");
  }
}

// required methods not implemented
```

```
public void ejbActivate() {}

public void ejbPassivate() {}

// business methods

public String getInterface() {
  return Interface;
}

public int getBandwidth() {
  return Bandwidth;
}

public String getServiceState() {
  return ServiceState;
}

// data base access methods required for bean-managed persistence
private void insertRow(id, Interface, Bandwidth, ServiceState) {
/* data-base-specific insert method must be included here */
}

private void deleteRow(id) {
/* data-base-specific delete method must be included here */
}

private void loadRow(id) {
/* data-base-specific load method must be included here */
}

private void storeRow(id) {
/* data-base-specific store method must be included here */
}

private boolean selectByPrimaryKey(primaryKey) {
/* data-base-specific select method must be included here */
}

}
```

Entity bean code (container-managed persistence)

Example Entity Bean - Configuration Manager (EquipEJB.java)

```java
import javax.ejb.*;

public class EquipEJB implements EntityBean {
  // the EJB create method for a container-managed persistence
  // Entity Bean returns null
  public String ejbCreate(String id, String Interface, int Bandwidth,
  String ServiceState)
    throws CreateException {

    if (id = = null) {
      throw new CreateException ("Equipment ID required.");
    }

    this.id = id;
    this.Interface = interface;
    this.Bandwidth = Bandwidth;
    this.ServiceState = ServiceState;

    return null;

  }

  // ejbPostCreate method must be included for each ejbCreate method
  public void ejbPostCreate(String id, String Interface,
  int Bandwidth, String ServiceState)
    throws CreateException {}

  // empty constructor
  public EquipEJB() {}

  // ejbRemove method is empty for container-managed persistence
  public void ejbRemove() {}

  // ejbLoad method is empty for container-managed persistence
  public void ejbLoad() {}

  // ejbStore method is empty for container-managed persistence
  public void ejbStore() {}

  // search by primary key not implemented
  public String ejbFindByPrimaryKey(String primaryKey) throws
  FinderException {}
```

```
// required methods not implemented
public void ejbActivate() {}

public void ejbPassivate() {}

// business methods

public String getInterface() {
  return Interface;
}

public int getBandwidth() {
  return Bandwidth;
}

public String getServiceState() {
  return ServiceState;
}
}
```

Home interface

The purpose of the home interface is to define the create methods that a client may invoke. The following code provides a home interface for the Equip entity bean.

```
import java.rmi.RemoteException;
import java.ejb.*;

public interface EquipHome extends EJBHome {

  public Equip create(String id, String Interface, int Bandwidth,
  String ServiceState)
    throws RemoteException, CreateException;

  public Equip findByPrimaryKey(String id)
    throws FinderException, RemoteException;

}
```

Remote interface

The remote interface defines the business methods that a client may invoke. The remote interface for the Equip entity bean is given below.

```
import javax.ejb.EJBObject;
import java.rmi.RemoteException;

public interface Equip extends EJBObject {

  public String getInterface() throws RemoteException;
  public int getBandwidth() throws RemoteException;
  public String getServiceState() throws RemoteException;
}
```

References

1. For an overview of telecommunications network management and protocol architecture, see Raman LG. Fundamentals of telecommunications network management. Piscataway, NJ: IEEE Press, 1999.

2. ITU-T M.3010. Principles of a telecommunications management network (TMN), November 1992.

3. ITU-T M.3100. Generic network information model, version 2, March 1995.

4. Case J, Fedor M, Schoffstall M, Davin J. IETF RFC 1157, simple network management protocol, May 1990.

5. Telcordia GR-831-CORE. Operations application messages: language for operations application messages. Telcordia November 1996;Issue 1.

6. ITU-T X.711. Common management information protocol, 1991.

7. Object Management Group. The common object request broker: architecture and specification. Framingham, MA: Object Management Group, 1998.

8. W3C Recommendation. Extensible markup language (XML) 1.0, second ed. 6 October 2000.

9. Java 2 platform enterprise edition, http://java.sun.com/j2ee/.

10. Enterprise Java Beans, http://java.sun.com/products/ejb/index.html.

11. Java Transaction Service, http://java.sun.com/products/jts/index.html.

12. Java Message Service, http://java.sun.com/products/jms/index.html.

13. Java Naming and Directory Interface, http://java.sun.com/products/jndi/index.html.

14. Java Server Pages, http://java.sun.com/products/jsp/index.html.

15. Bea Weblogic E-Business Platform, http://www.bea.com/about/platform.shtml.

16. IBM Websphere Application Servers, http://www-4.ibm.com/software/webservers/appserv/.

17. iPlanet Java Application Server, http://www.iplanet.com/products/infrastructure/app-servers/.

6

XML and Java for telecommunications

Thomas C. Jepsen

Programming Languages Editor, IT Professonal, USA

6.1 What is XML?

Extensible markup language, or XML, is a language for describing markup languages. It provides a facility for defining tags and the relationships between them. XML is similar to HTML but provides more generality; unlike HTML, which has fixed tag definitions, XML allows users to define application-specific tags. XML is a subset of standard generalized markup language, or SGML. It is being developed and standardized by the World Wide Web Consortium (W3C), an international consortium of companies and academic institutions tasked with developing open standards for Internet web applications.

6.1.1 Advantages of XML

XML provides a standard means of exchanging information between applications, between business partners, and between businesses and consumers. It enables interoperability in e-commerce and Internet applications. Specific markup languages can be developed for specific industries and applications – for example, the Real

Estate Transaction Service (RETS) has been developed for real estate transactions [1]. The chemical industry has developed the chemical markup language, or CML [2]. And the telecommunications industry is in the process of developing the telecommunications markup language, or tML [3].

The W3C's 10 (actually seven) points, which can be found on the W3C website (*http://www.w3.org/*) provide a good summary of XML and its uses:

- *XML is a method for putting structured data in a text file*. Structured data is data organized in a specific, often hierarchical format, such as an address, or a spreadsheet entry.

- *XML looks a bit like HTML, but isn't HTML*. XML uses tags and attributes that appear similar to those used in HTML. However, unlike HTML tags, which have fixed meanings, XML tags are user-defined.

- *XML is text, but isn't meant to be read*. While XML uses text encoding, most XML is intended for program-to-program communication, rather than for human-to-machine communication.

- *XML is a family of technologies*. The XML 1.0 specification, released by the W3C in 1998, is the basic definition of XML, but many additional modules of functionality have been developed and standardized by the W3C.

- *XML is verbose, but that is not a problem*. Since text encoding is less efficient than binary encoding, XML files always take up more space than equivalent binary files. However, given the readability advantages of text files and the ready availability of compression algorithms, this is not seen as a major problem in practical applications.

- *XML is new, but not that new*. XML standardization began in 1996; the XML 1.0 specification was released by the W3C in February 1998. XML is based on HTML, which was developed in the early 1990s, and SGML, which was developed in the 1980s.

- *XML is license-free, platform-independent, and well-supported*. As a W3C-developed technology, XML does not require licensing, and it comes with a wide variety of supporting tools and applications.

6.1.2 *The W3C XML 1.0 Recommendation*

The defining specification for XML is the W3C's *Extensible Markup Language (XML) 1.0 (Second Edition) W3C Recommendation*, 6 October 2000 [4]. This specification, first released in February 1998 and re-issued with corrections in October 2000, defines XML as a subset of SGML, as defined in the International Standards Organization (ISO) 8879:1986(E) specification.

The basic concept of XML is that of a *document*. A document in XML is made up of storage units called *entities*, which contain either parsed or unparsed data. Parsed data is in turn made up of *characters*, some of which form character data, and some of which form *markup*. Markup encodes a description of the document's storage layout and logical structure. An XML-aware application uses an XML processor to read XML documents and provide access to their content and structure.

To be recognized as an XML document, a data object must be *well-formed*. Being well-formed simply means that the document follows all the rules set out in W3C XML 1.0. In addition, a document may be *valid* if it meets certain additional requirements specified by a validating entity, such as a *document type definition* (DTD).

A document contains elements that are delimited by start tags and end tags. Start and end tags are types of markup, as are entity references, character references, comments, DTDs, and CDATA. (CDATA sections are used to escape blocks of data containing characters that would otherwise be treated as markup.) Thus an XML document consists primarily of character data in the form of elements, with markup tags to indicate their beginning and ending points.

An XML document begins with a prolog statement that indicates the version of XML to which it refers:

```
<?xml version = "1.0"?>
```

Currently, "1.0" is the only valid version number. A complete well-formed XML document can be created by simply adding tags and character data, e.g.

```
<?xml version = "1.0"?>
<statement> Hello World!</statement >
```

An XML processor can recognize this object as a well-formed XML document, since it consists of character types and markup defined in W3C XML 1.0. However, it cannot determine if the document is valid, since it has no validating entity to refer to. In order to validate the document, the processor must be able to refer to a DTD that contains the markup declarations for the document. (In the above example, the DTD would identify <statement> and </statement> as valid markup tags.) There are several ways to refer to a DTD; one way would be to include a reference to an external DTD in the prolog:

```
<?xml version = "1.0"?>
<!DOCTYPE HelloWorld SYSTEM
http://www.hello.com/HelloWorld.dtd>
<statement> Hello World! </statement>
```

The HelloWorld.dtd would contain a markup declaration which would contain the grammar for the markup tag used in the document:

```
<!ELEMENT statement (#PCDATA)>
```

The concept of the DTD is inherited from SGML; as in SGML, the DTD is a non-XML document and uses a different syntax. DTDs are limited in their ability to perform data typing; this and other limitations of the DTD approach have led to the effort to develop *schemas* for use in XML document validation (see below).

XML normally uses the hypertext transfer protocol (HTTP) for transport; however, use of HTTP is not a requirement, and any protocol capable of transporting text-encoded data may be used.

6.2 Tools for XML presentation and display

XML may be used for presentation and display of data to human users, similar to the use of HTML in web pages. However, since XML does not have tags with fixed display and formatting characteristics, a *style sheet language* must be used to specify formatting and display properties. Two common style sheet languages are cascading style sheets and extensible stylesheet language; each is described below.

6.2.1 Cascading style sheets (CSS)

CSS is a style sheet language that enables document creators to attach style specifications to structured HTML and XML documents. It is applicable to XML in applications where XML is used for document display in web pages, and may also be applied to presentation in other media (e.g. speech synthesis). The defining specification for CSS is *the Cascading Style Sheets, Level 2 CSS2 Specification*, W3C Recommendation, 12 May 1998 [5].

CSS separates the presentation style of a document from the content, thus simplifying document creation and maintenance. Separate style sheets are created which specify presentation attributes of document elements. If a document is to be rendered as a web page, the style sheet might specify font size, font style, or color for individual document elements. The CSS specification assumes the use of user agents to prepare documents for display. For example, a user agent might do the following:

- Parse the source document and create a document tree;
- Identify the target media type;
- Retrieve all style sheets associated with the document that are specified for the target media type;
- Annotate every element of the document tree by assigning a single value to every property that is applicable to the target media type.

CSS provides a simple and easy-to-learn style sheet capability for non-complex document presentation. For applications which require text generation or transformation, XSL and XSLT are generally more appropriate.

6.2.2 Extensible stylesheet language/XSL transformations (XSL/XSLT)

XSL is a language for expressing style sheets which builds upon the CSS approach. It consists of two parts: a language for transforming XML documents; and an XML vocabulary for specifying formatting semantics. The defining document for XSL is the *Extensible Stylesheet Language (XSL) Version 1.0 W3C Candidate Recommendation*, 21 November 2000 [6].

An XSL style sheet specifies the presentation of an XML document by describing how the document is transformed into an XML document that uses the formatting vocabulary described in the XSL specification. A document designer uses an XSL style sheet to show how structured content should be presented, i.e. how the content should be styled, laid out, and paginated into some presentation medium, such as a window in a web browser or hand-held device.

XSL provides an extensible model for pagination and layout that supports both scrollable document windows and pagination, in order to give designers control over the features needed when documents are paginated as well as to provide an equivalent frame-based structure for browsing on the Web. An XSL style sheet processor is used to produce XML presentation, using an XML source document and an XSL style sheet as input. Since element names have no "built-in" presentation semantics in XML as they do in HTML, a processor does not know how to present a document unless a style sheet is used. To produce presentation content, the processor first constructs a result tree from the XML source, and then interprets the result tree to produce formatted results. This transformation process allows the presented document to appear significantly different from the original source document. For example, a table of contents could be added, or data could be displayed as a formatted list.

Formatting objects are included in the result tree in order to perform formatting. Formatting objects consist of standard document presentation attributes, such as a page or a paragraph. Formatting properties permit a higher granularity of control to be applied, such as word spacing or indentation.

The process of constructing the result tree is referred to as tree transformation. The tree transformation process is described in *XSL Transformations (XSLT) Version 1.0 W3C Recommendation*, 16 November 1999 [7].

The result tree can be output as an XML document containing formatting objects. This can be used directly by some applications to serve client-specific data; for example, wireless application protocol (WAP) servers can use this technique to prepare input for hand-held devices [8].

6.2.3 Wireless Markup Language (WML)

WML is an XML-based markup language designed to be used with WAP for content presentation on a wireless terminal. The WAP platform is an open specification that is intended to standardize the way wireless devices (mobile phones, personal digital assistants, etc.) access Internet data and services [9]. The small screen area available and the limited amount of computing power available in most handheld devices creates special requirements for information presentation and display. To support the special requirements of WAP-enabled handheld devices, a WAP gateway is employed to translate between WAP-based wireless devices and HTTP-based content servers. Figure 6.1 shows the network architecture for WAP-based devices.

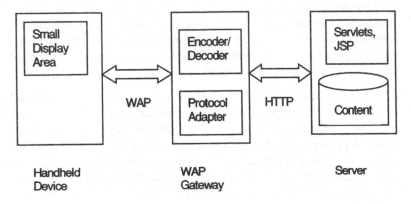

Figure 6.1 *WAP architecture for wireless applications.*

Because HTML is not well-suited for small-screen devices, the WAP standard defines its own markup language, WML. WML is defined as a specific XML DTD with the following distinguishing characteristics:

- WML is specifically designed for wireless terminals which have display areas of about 1 inch (2.5 cm.) width capable of displaying only a few lines of text;

- WML is case-sensitive; all tags and attributes should be lower-case;

- WML is not as error-tolerant as HTML;

- WML does not assume that a standard computer input device, such as a full keyboard or mouse, is available for data input.

The basic unit of display information for WML is the "card," which represents a single user interaction. A simple card example (example.wml) is given below:

```
<?xml version = "1.0"?>
<!DOCTYPE wml PUBLIC "- / /WAPFORUM/ /DTD WML 1.1/ /EN"
http://www.wapforum.org/DTD/wml_1.1.xml>
```

```
<wml>
  <card id = "MyFirstCard" title = "First Card">
    <p align = "center">
      Hello World!
    </p>
  </card>
</wml>
```

The prolog in example.wml specifies a WML DTD for validation, pointed to by the URL *http://www.wapforum.org/DTD/wml_1.1.xml*. If viewed on a WAP-enabled hand-held device, this WML card would display the title "First Card," followed by the text message "Hello World!"

Using servlets and JSPs with WML

WML can be generated by servlets in much the same manner as HTML. An example servlet to generate the text of the example.wml card (WmlHelloWorld.java) is shown below.

```
import java.io.*;
import javax.servlet.*;
import javax.servlet.http.*;

/**
* This servlet displays the message "hello world" on a
  wireless handheld device.
*/

public class WmlHelloWorld extends HttpServlet {

public void service (HttpServletRequest request,
  HttpServletResponse response)
throws ServletException, IOException {
  // set content type for wireless data
  response.setContentType("text/vnd.wap.wml");

  //create PrintWriter object to communicate with
  requesting client
  PrintWriter out = response.getWriter();

  //write data
  out.println("<?xml version = \"1.0\"?>");
  out.println("<!DOCTYPE wml PUBLIC \"- / /WAPFORUM/ /DTD
    WML 1.1/ /EN\"");
```

```
out.println(" \http://www.wapforum.org/DTD/
  wml_1.1.xml \ ">");
out.println("<wml>");
out.println("<card title = \"First Card\">");
out.println("<p align = \"center\">");
out.println("Hello World!");
out.println("</p>");
out.println("</card>");
out.println("</wml>");
  }
}
```

A Java server page (JSP) to perform the same function (WmlHelloWorld.jsp) is even simpler:

```
<?xml version = "1.0"?>
<!DOCTYPE wml PUBLIC "- / /WAPFORUM/ /DTD WML 1.1/ /EN"
http://www.wapforum.org/DTD/wml_1.1.xml>

<%
response.setContentType("text/vnd.wap.wml");
out.println("<wml>");
out.println("<card title = \"First Card\">");
out.println("<p align = \"center\">");
out.println("Hello World!");
out.println("</p>");
out.println("</card>");
out.println("</wml>");
%>
```

Note that for both the servlet and the JSP, the MIME type ("text/vnd.wap.wml") must be set correctly for the WML document [10].

6.3 Tools for application-to-application messaging

The primary use that has emerged for XML is in application-to-application messaging. For example, to complete a business transaction, a customer data entry application may format customer data entry into an XML document, and pass it to another application that is responsible for processing the order. The structure of an XML document is defined by the W3C document object model (DOM). Operations may then be performed on the entire document, or on individual elements and attributes of the document, in order to complete the business transaction.

There are two major types of XML application programming interfaces (APIs): a *tree-based* API compiles an XML document into an internal tree structure, then allows an application to navigate that tree. The DOM is a tree-based API. An *event-based* API, on the other hand, reports parsing events (such as the start and end of elements) directly to the application through callbacks, and does not usually build an internal tree. The simple API for XML (SAX) is an event-based API.

6.3.1 Document object model (DOM)

DOM is an API for HTML and XML documents. It defines the logical structure of a document, and the manner in which the document may be accessed and manipulated. The DOM may be used to build documents, navigate their structure, and perform add/modify/delete operations on elements and content. The DOM which is applicable to XML is defined in the *Document Object Model (DOM) Level 1 Specification Version 1.0 W3C Recommendation*, 1 October 1998 [11], and in the recently updated version, *Document Object Model (DOM) Level 2 Core Specification Version 1.0 W3C Recommendation*, 13 November 2000 [12].

The DOM specification is divided into two parts: Core and HTML. The Level 1 Core section defines a low-level set of fundamental interfaces that can represent any structured document, and extended interfaces for representing an XML document. The Level 2 Core specification adds support for namespaces (see below).

The DOM presents documents as a hierarchy of node objects. Some nodes permit child nodes, while others are leaf nodes that do not permit child nodes. Table 6.1 lists node objects and their permitted child nodes.

The DOM also specifies a **NodeList** interface to handle ordered lists of Nodes (such as the children of a node) and a **NamedNodeMap** interface to handle unordered sets of nodes, referenced by their name attribute, such as attributes of an Element. Changes to the underlying document structure are immediately reflected in all **NodeList**s and **NamedNodeMap**s.

Table 6.1 Document object model (DOM) 1.0: node objects and permitted child nodes

Node object	Permitted child nodes	Description
Document	Element (maximum 1), ProcessingInstruction, Comment, DocumentType	The document interface represents the entire XML document. It is the root of the document tree, and provides the primary access to the document's data
DocumentFragment	Element, ProcessingInstruction, Comment, Text, CDATASection, EntityReference	A "lightweight" or "minimal" document object
DocumentType	None	Provides an interface to the list of entities that are defined for the document

Table 6.1 (*continued*)

Node object	Permitted child nodes	Description
EntityReference	Element, ProcessingInstruction, Comment, Text, CDATASection, EntityReference	May be inserted into the structure model when an entity reference is in the source document, or when the user wishes to insert an entity reference
Element	Element, Text, Comment, ProcessingInstruction, CDATASection, EntityReference	Most objects encountered when traversing a document are element nodes. Element nodes may have attributes associated with them
Attr	Text, EntityReference	Represents an attribute in an element object. Typically the allowable values for the attribute are defined in a document type definition
ProcessingInstruction	None	Represents a "processing instruction", used in XML as a way to keep processor-specific information in the text of the document
Comment	None	Represents the content of a comment, i.e. all the characters between the starting "<!–" and ending "–>"
Text	None	Represents the textual content (termed character data in XML) of an element or Attr.
CDATASection	None	Used to escape blocks of text containing characters that would otherwise be regarded as markup
Entity	Element, ProcessingInstruction, Comment, Text, CDATASection, EntityReference	Represents an entity, either parsed or unparsed, in an XML document
Notation	None	Represents a notation declared in the DTD

6.3.2 Namespaces

XML documents may contain elements and attributes that are defined in, and used by, multiple software modules. To enable multiple markup vocabularies to co-exist in the same document without causing confusion, the concept of the *namespace* was developed by the W3C. A namespace is defined as a collection of names, identified by a Universal Resource Identifier (URI), which are used in XML documents as element types and attribute names. Namespaces and their use in XML documents are defined in the *Namespaces in XML W3C Recommendation*, 14 January 1999 [13].

Namespace declarations are indicated in XML documents with the prefix "xmlns:." In the "time" element example given below, the prefix "tat" is bound to the URI *http://www.timeandtemp.com/schema* for the time element and its contents.

```
<time xmlns:tat = 'http://www.timeandtemp.com
  /schema'>
</time>
```

The actual use of the URI referenced by the namespace declaration is application dependent. The W3C metadata standard, *Resource Description Framework Model and Syntax Specification W3C Recommendation*, 22 February 1999 [14], uses the URI to point to a file which provides typing information for each element. Thus, namespaces play an important role in referencing schemas for validation (see description of schemas below.)

6.3.3 Schemas

The XML 1.0 Recommendation provides for validation of elements and attributes by means of DTDs. However, DTDs do not provide data typing, and thus allow ambiguity in element and attribute declaration. To remedy this, the W3C has recently completed work on schema definitions, which provide for typing and therefore permit more precise validation of XML elements and attributes. Schemas for XML are defined in *XML Schema Part 0: Primer, W3C Recommendation*, 2 May 2001; *XML Schema Part 1: Structures, W3C Recommendation*, 2 May 2001; and *XML Schema Part 2: Datatypes, W3C Recommendation*, 2 May 2001 [15–17].

An XML schema consists of a set of schema components. The primary components are:

- Simple type definitions
- Complex type definitions
- Element declarations
- Attribute declarations

Elements in XML may be of *simple* or *complex* types. An element which contains subelements or attributes is a complex type; an element which consists of a simple value (e.g. string or integer) is a simple type. Attributes by definition are always simple types.

An example XML document, so.xml, which might be used in the telecommunications industry for customer service orders is shown below:

```
<?xml version = "1.0"?>
<ServiceOrder orderDate = "2001-02-28">
  <ServiceAddress>
    <name>Arthur Smith</name>
    <street>100 Main Street</street>
    <city>Davenport</city>
    <state>IA</state>
```

```
      <zip>52806</zip>
    </ServiceAddress>
    <BillingAddress>
      <name>Jane Smith</name>
      <street>400 Jones Street</street>
      <city>Davenport</city>
      <state>IA</state>
      <zip>52806</zip>
    </BillingAddress>
    </TypeofService>
      <ServiceCategory>adsl</ServiceCategory>
      <ServiceLevel>Premium</ServiceLevel>
      <BandWidth>1000</BandWidth>
    </TypeofService>
  </ServiceOrder>
```

This example service order document, which might be used to order a telecommunications service, consists of a service order element which in turn consists of three subelements: a service address element, a billing address element, and a type of service element. The service order element is a complex type, since it contains subelements. Each of the three subelements is also complex, since each contains subelements.

An example schema for the above XML document, so.xsd, is shown below:

```
<xsd:schema xmlns:xsd = "http://www.w3.org/2000/08/
   XMLSchema">

  <xsd:annotation>
    <xsd:documentation>
      Service order schema for Telco.com.
      Copyright 2000 Telco.com.
    </xsd:documentation>
  </xsd:annotation>

  <xsd:element name = "ServiceOrder" type =
    "ServiceOrderType"/>

  <xsd:complexType name = "ServiceOrderType">
    <xsd:sequence>
      <xsd:element name = "ServiceAddress" type =
        "USAddress"/>
      <xsd:element name = "BillingAddress" type =
        "USAddress"/>
      <xsd:element name =
        "TypeofService" type = "TypeofService"/>
```

```
    </xsd:sequence>
    <xsd:attribute name = "orderDate" type =
      "xsd:date"/>
  </xsd:complexType>

  <xsd:complexType name = "USAddress">
    <xsd:sequence>
      <xsd:element name = "name" type = "xsd:string"/>
      <xsd:element name = "street" type = "xsd:string"/>
      <xsd:element name = "city" type = "xsd:string"/>
      <xsd:element name = "state" type = "xsd:string"/>
      <xsd:element name = "zip" type = "xsd:decimal"/>
    </xsd:sequence>
  </xsd:complexType>

  <xsd:complexType name = "TypeofService">
    <xsd:sequence>
      <xsd:element name = "ServiceCategory" type =
        "xsd:string"/>
      <xsd:element name = "ServiceLevel" type =
        "xsd:string"/>
      <xsd:element name = "BandWidth" type =
        "xsd:decimal"/>
    </xsd:sequence>
  </xsd:complexType>

</xsd:schema>
```

The first line in the schema is a namespace declaration which specifies that the prefix "xsd" is associated with the W3C XML schema namespace. Thus, everything in the schema that is prefixed by xsd: (for example, xsd:element) is a data item that is defined in the W3C schema referenced by the namespace declaration. This provides the first level of inheritance and ties this schema (so.xsd) to the W3C standard by associating elements and simple types with the W3C schema standard. The namespace declaration is followed by an annotation which provides documentation of the schema, identifies its purpose, and includes a copyright notice.

The element declaration following the annotation defines the service order element as a "service order type." The next eight lines declare the service order type to be a complexType element consisting of three subelements: service address, billing address, and type of service. The service order type also contains an order date attribute, which consists of the simple type "date." Since service address and billing address use the same format, the same complex type format, US address, may be used for both. The US address complex type declaration specifies the five simple type elements that comprise a US address: a name string, a street string, a city string, a state string, and a decimal zip code. Finally, the type of service element is defined as a complex type consisting of three simple elements: a service category string, a service level string, and a decimal bandwidth specification.

Note that the service order XML document (so.xml) does not contain an explicit reference to the schema (so.xsd) which declares its elements and attributes. The W3C XML schema specification does not require that an explicit reference to a schema be contained within an XML document; however, it is often useful to do so. One way to provide an explicit reference is to include a namespace declaration for the schema, for example, the second line in so.xml could be changed from

```
<ServiceOrder orderDate = "2001-02-28">
```

to

```
<ServiceOrder xmlns = "http://www.telco.com/so"
  orderDate = "2001-02-28">
```

The XML Schema, Part 0, Primer provides additonal information on namespace declarations for schemas [15].

6.4 Java and XML

Java and XML have evolved as complementary technologies. Both were designed with platform independence as a primary goal, and applications that use both take advantage of this natural synergy by combining Java's platform-independent executables with XML's platform-independent data. Many of the applications which have been developed for generating and manipulating XML are Java based, and the W3C specifies a Java-language API as part of the DOM specification.

6.4.1 DOM and SAX

Two basic approaches to manipulating XML documents using Java have been developed. One is based on the DOM API and involves operations performed upon the document as a tree structure. Figure 6.2 shows the service order example discussed above (so.xml) represented as a DOM tree structure. An XML processor using the DOM API will generate a document tree consisting of all the elements and attributes in the document, and present the entire document to an application for processing. This approach is well suited for applications which must perform operations on the whole document; an example would be an application which moves elements from one location in the document to another.

Another approach to XML document processing is based on the simple API for XML (SAX), a public domain API developed by members of the XML-DEV list

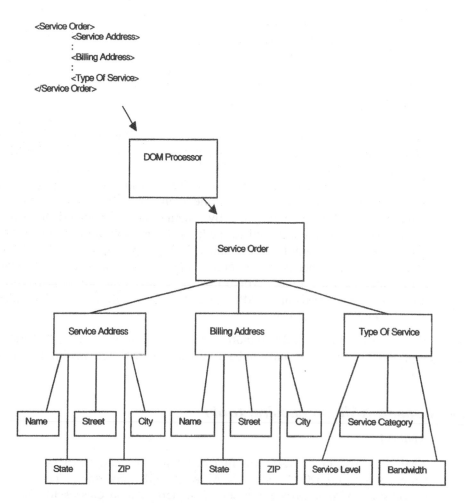

Figure 6.2 *XML document tree structure using DOM.*

[18]. This approach uses events and event handlers to perform actions based on individual document elements. An XML processor, or *parser*, based on the SAX model would produce a series of event notifications similar to the following example upon reading in the service order document, and present them to an application:

```
StartElement: ServiceOrder
StartElement: ServiceAddress
StartElement: name
Characters: Arthur Smith
EndElement: name
StartElement: street
Characters: 100 Main Street
EndElement: street
```

```
StartElement: city
Characters: Davenport
EndElement: city
  :
  :
EndElement: ServiceOrder
```

The action taken by the application upon notification of a start of element or end of element notification is totally up to the application; the SAX API merely provides the event mechanism. Parsers may be *validating* or *non-validating*. A non-validating parser simply generates events to indicate the start or end of an element, while a validating parser checks to see if the element corresponds to the definition contained in a DTD or pointed to by a namespace. A non-validating parser can determine if a document is well-formed; however, a validating parser is required to determine if a document is valid. Using a SAX parser is appropriate for applications that do not require access to the entire document, or for cases where placing the entire document in memory would use up too much memory. SAX is sometimes referred to as a "read-only" API, since it does not allow the user to generate or modify an XML document.

Version 1 of the SAX API supports validation by means of DTDs; version 2 adds support of namespaces, and can be used with the W3C schema implementation for validation.

6.4.2 Java-based XML processing tools

XML4J

XML for Java, or XML4J, was first developed by IBM Corporation in 1998. It supports both the DOM and SAX APIs for XML processing. To perform DOM processing, XML4J provides a set of implementation classes for the interfaces specified in the W3C DOM 1.0 API. To generate a new XML document using the XML4J API, you must first create an instance of TXDocument, the XML4J implementation of the DOM 1.0 Document interface:

```
import org.W3C.dom.Document;
import com.ibm.xml.parser.TXDocument;
  :
Document so = new TXDocument();
```

Additional XML4J implementations of the DOM1.0 API interfaces may be used to create elements and add them to the document. For example, to add the ServiceOrder element to the so document created above as the root element, the following class implementations would be used:

```
Element root = new TXElement("ServiceOrder");
so.appendChild(root);
```

Subelements may be added to the root element in a similar fashion:

```
Element item = so.createElement("ServiceAddress");
root.appendChild(item);
```

By recursively creating and adding elements in this manner, it is possible to generate an entire XML document using the XML4J class implementations. (see Section 6.6 for a sample XML4J program which generates the so.xml document.)

Early versions of XML4J supported DOM Level 1 and SAX Version 1 only, and did not support use of schemas. The most recent versions of XML4J support DOM Level 2, SAX Version 2, and a preliminary implementation of schemas [19].

JAXP

The Java API for XML Parsing, or JAXP, was developed as part of the Java Community Process to provide a standardized set of Java platform APIs for parsing and manipulating XML documents. While the SAX and DOM APIs provide much useful functionality, they also require that the user have detailed knowledge of the processor implementation. The JAXP API provides a "pluggability" mechanism that abstracts the details of SAX or DOM processor implementation by means of a `javax.xml.parsers` API [20].

Separate implementations are provided for the SAX and DOM APIs. For the SAX API, a **SAXParserFactory** is used to create an instance of **SAXParser**. The **SAXParserFactory** can be configured to create parsers that are namespace aware, validating, or both. The following example code creates a SAX parser that is both namespace aware and validating:

```
SAXParser parser;
HandlerBase handler = new MyApplicationHandlerBase();
SAXParserFactory factory =
  SAXParserFactory.newInstance();
factory.setNamespaceAware(true);
factory.setValidating(true);
try {
  parser = factory.newSAXParser();
  parser.parse(http://www.telco.com/so.xml, handler);
} catch (SAXException se) {
  // handle error
} catch (IOException ioe) {
  //handle error
} catch (ParserConfigurationException pce) {
  //handle error
}
```

JAXP1.0 provides the SAX 1.0 parser as the default parser. However, users may use a different parser by setting a system property (javax.xml.parsers.SAXParserFactory) to a different parser.

To support the DOM API, JAXP uses a **DocumentBuilder** instance which provides a wrapper for the underlying DOM entities. Similar to the SAX API, the user must first instantiate an instance of a **DocumentBuilderFactory**, which in turn is used to create an instance of **DocumentBuilder**. The JAXP implementation of the DOM API uses SAX API classes to read in XML data and construct the DOM tree of data objects. The following example code creates a DOM parser that is both namespace aware and validating:

```
DocumentBuilder builder;
DocumentBuilderFactory factory = DocumentBuilderFactory.newInstance();
factory.setNamespaceAware(true);
factory.setValidating(true);
String location = http://www.telco.com/so.xml;
try {
  builder = factory.newDocumentBuilder();
  Document document = builder.parse(location);
} catch (SAXException se) {
  // handle error
} catch (IOException ioe) {
  //handle error
} catch (ParserConfigurationException pce) {
  //handle error
}
```

The Apache XML project

The Apache XML project has produced a number of open-standards XML tools, including several Java-based parsers [21]. The Xerces Java Parser, Release 1.3.0, supports schemas, DOM Level 2 Version 1.0, and SAX Version 2, in addition to DOM Level 1 and SAX Version 1. Crimson is a small-footprint Java parser which supports XML 1.0; it is the default parser for JAXP 1.1.

XML data binding

A Java Community Process project, codenamed "Adelard," is currently in the process of developing a specification for XML data binding. This specification would allow schemas to be translated directly into Java classes that may in turn be used for parsing, validation, and document generation. This approach is particularly suitable for applications where intensive validation is required, such as e-commerce servers. Compiling schemas into Java classes, rather than interpreting

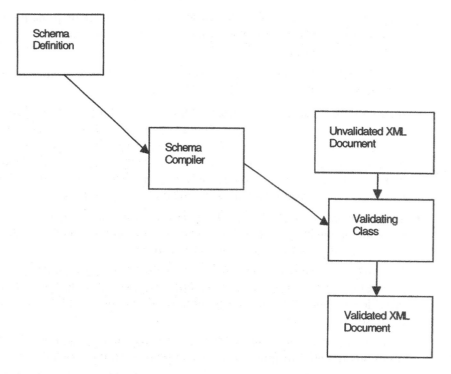

Figure 6.3 *Schema compiler for data binding.*

them at runtime, yields performance improvements and reduces the memory footprint required for validation [22]. Figure 6.3 shows the use of a schema compiler for data binding.

6.5 XML in telecommunications

XML is particularly well suited for use in telecommunications management systems. Network management systems use a wide variety of proprietary and incompatible protocols and messaging formats to transfer information from one component to another. Using XML to replace these proprietary messaging formats not only simplifies management functions, but makes true interoperability among operations systems possible.

6.5.1 Background

In order to provide a common architecture for management systems, and to ensure compatibility in multi-vendor environments, the ITU-T began to develop the concept of the telecommunications management network (TMN) in 1988. The goal of this work was to provide an architecture and set of principles to allow interoperability between network elements (NEs) and network management systems (NMS), and among NMS.

ITU-T M.3010, *Telecommunications Management Network*, abstracts TMN architecture into a set of hierarchical levels [23]:

- *Business management level (BML).* This is the highest level of abstraction and addresses enterprise objectives. This is the level which is least susceptible to standardization, since business functions are driven by market needs and enterprise-specific considerations. This is the level which addresses the basic business goals of the enterprise, such as billing customers for services provided and making business arrangements with other service providers.

- *Service management level (SML).* The service management level abstracts network operation into a set of service specifications which detail the grades and levels of service provided to each customer.

- *Network management level (NML).* The network management level provides an abstraction of the end-to-end connections required across the network in order to provide services, and provides monitoring of the functionality and performance of these connections.

- *Element management level (EML).* The element management level abstracts the functions required to implement and support customer services at the network element level, such as provisioning interface cards and providing physical connections to the end user.

- *Element level (EL).* This is the level at which network elements provide services to customers by means of physical components such as interface cards and terminations.

Additionally, the TMN specifications define a set of functional components, sometimes referred to as "FCAPS," which define generic functional areas related to network management. FCAPS consists of *fault management* (alarm surveillance, fault isolation, and testing); *configuration management* (provisioning, status and control, and installation); *performance management* (performance monitoring, traffic management, and quality of service); *security management* (service authorization, user validation, encryption/decryption); and *accounting management* (usage metering and billing). It is possible to construct a useful TMN model for design purposes by building a matrix of levels and the FCAPS functions performed by each level.

The TMN specifications also define interfaces among network elements and abstract levels of management. A *Q interface* can be thought of as a "vertical" interface between an operations system (OS) and a network element, or between two levels of an OS within the same TMN. An *X interface* is a "horizontal" interface between two peer OS layers in different TMNs. Thus a Q interface might be used to transfer provisioning instructions from an element management level to a network element, or to report alarm events from the network element to the element manager. An X interface might be used to transfer service definitions or billing information between two TMNs which jointly provide services to a single user [24].

A wide variety of messaging formats and protocols are currently in use for performing network management functions. The original TMN standards define an application layer service called the common management information service element (CMISE), and its accompanying protocol, the common management information protocol (CMIP) [25]. CMISE/CMIP uses an information model based on the Guidelines for the Definition of Managed Objects (GDMO) and the Abstract Syntax Notation One (ASN.1) [26]. The Internet Engineering Task Force (IETF) has developed the simple network management protocol (SNMP) and an associated management information base (MIB) for Internet-related network management [27]. The Object Management Group (OMG) specifies the common object request broker architecture (CORBA), which may be applied to telecommunications

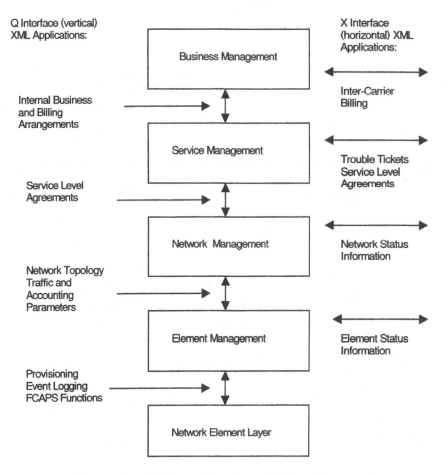

Figure 6.4 *TMN network model and XML applications.*

network management [28]. And many network management applications use versions of transaction language one (TL1), an ASCII-based man-machine language standardized by Bellcore (now Telcordia) [29].

While each of these management protocols and information models has technical and operational advantages, each also has drawbacks that have prevented any of them from achieving a dominant position in the network management field. Some are complex and slow; others do not scale well, and many exist only as proprietary vendor-specific implementations. Using XML files to perform transfer of network management information between managed elements and management components provides a solution that is simple, scaleable, and interoperable. Figure 6.4

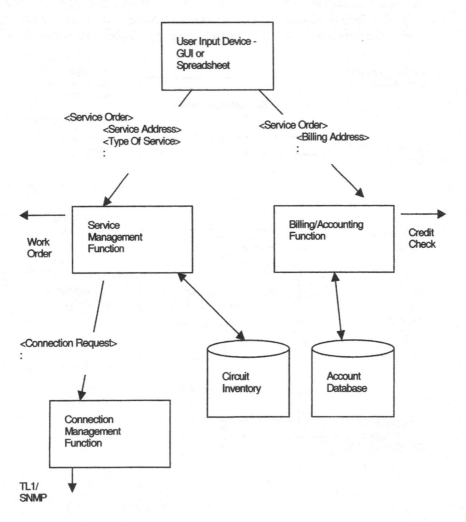

Figure 6.5   *Example of service order application using XML.*

shows potential applications for XML in the TMN architectural model for both X and Q interfaces.

As an example of a telecommunications customer service order application, the customer service order XML document described above (so.xml) can be generated by extracting information from fields on a graphical user interface (GUI), or produced from spreadsheet entries. The document may then be transferred to a billing/accounting function, where a parser detects the billing address elements and initiates creation of a new account for the billed customer. (The information could also be used to generate a request to an external system for a credit check.)

The same service order document could be sent to a service management function, where a parser could detect the service address, and initiate a database lookup to determine if the service requested by the type of service element is available at the service address. If so, the information could be used to initiate a connection request for the specified service address; if not, the service manager could initiate a work order request to install the resources necessary to support the specified service.

The connection request itself could be implemented in a device-independent manner by means of an XML file. A device-independent XML file containing the necessary connection setup parameters could be sent to the proper network or element managers; the network/element managers could use a parser to generate vendor- or device-specific TL1 or SNMP commands to set up the connection in the network elements. Figure 6.5 illustrates the use of XML in the example service order function.

6.5.2 Standardization

Network management applications must be able to interoperate at all levels of the network hierarchy. This means that local exchange carriers must be able to interoperate with long-haul or interexchange carriers, and interexchange carriers must be able to interoperate with each other at an international level. Providing the necessary DTDs and/or schemas to ensure this interoperability for XML applications will require close coordination among standards bodies. DTDs and schemas must be made available for validation through *repositories*; if an application does not know the location of a specific repository, it should be able to look up the repository in a *registry* maintained by a standards organization.

Standardization work is currently being carried on by a number of organizations. In the US, the T1M1 Standards Committee for Internetwork Operations, Administration, Maintenance and Provisioning, is developing the *Telecommunications Markup Language (tML) Framework Document*, which provides a framework for development of schemas. Figure 6.6 shows the relationship of the proposed framework document to a complete tML specification. The ITU-T Study Group 4 has begun standardization work on XML for telecommunications jointly with the T1M1 Standards Committee. It is anticipated that ITU-T SG4 will concentrate

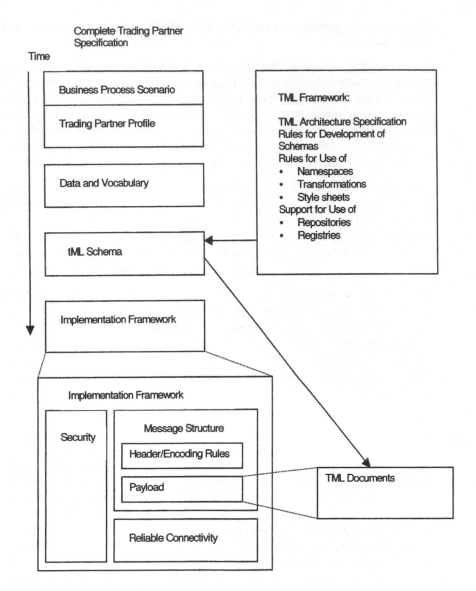

Figure 6.6 *Relationship of tML framework document to complete specification.*

on development of standards for applications which require interoperability at the international level, and relegate national issues to groups such as the T1M1 working group in the US.

6.5.3 Electronic business XML initiative (ebXML)

ebXML is an effort to standardize electronic business transactions. ebXML is jointly sponsored by the United Nations Centre for Trade Facilitation and Electronic Business (UN/CEFACT) [30] and the Organization for the Advancement of Structured Information Standards (OASIS) [31]. The purpose of the initiative is to make the benefits of electronic business transactions available to small and medium businesses. While ebXML is not intended specifically for telecommunications applications, it is well suited for business arrangements among international carriers, telecommunications service providers, and equipment vendors. Architecture and fundamental principles of ebXML are described in the *ebXML Technical Architecture Specification* [32]. Figure 6.7 shows how a company can build an ebXML implementation, store scenario information in a registry, and engage in a business transaction with a trading partner.

In the example shown, Company A requests business details from a known repository to determine requirements for participation in ebXML-compliant transac-

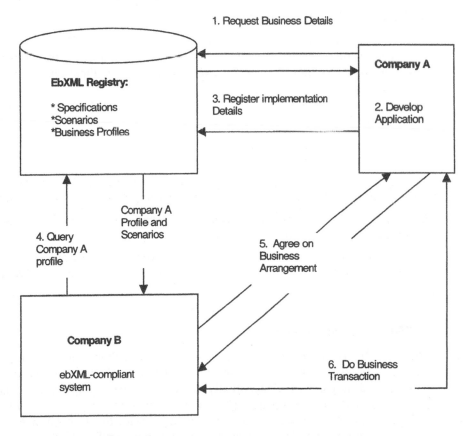

Figure 6.7   *Business transaction model using ebXML.*

tions (Step 1). Company A decides to create its own implementation, either through software development or by purchasing a turnkey application (Step 2). It submits its implementation details, reference links, and a trading partner profile, including sample business scenarios, to the registry (Step 3). Company B wishes to conduct a business transaction with Company A using standard ebXML software. It first queries the registry to obtain Company A's profile and business scenarios (Step 4), and then agrees on a business arrangement directly with Company A after determining that Company A is capable of performing the transaction (Step 5). Company A and Company B are then ready to engage in ebXML-compliant business transactions (Step 6).

The business model example described above uses the following concepts and architectural components:

1. A standard mechanism for describing a *business process* and its associated information model;

2. A mechanism for registering and storing a business process and its associated information model, so that it can be shared and reused;

3. Discovery of information about each participant, including:
   - The business processes they support;
   - The business service interfaces they offer in support of the business process;
   - The business messages to be exchanged between their respective service interfaces;
   - The technical configuration of the supported security, transport, and encoding protocols;

4. A mechanism for registering the aforementioned information so that it may be discovered and retrieved;

5. A mechanism for describing a trading partner agreement (TPA) which may be derived from the information about each participant from item 3 above;

6. A standardized messaging service which enables interoperable, secure, and reliable exchange of messages between two parties;

7. A mechanism for configuration of the respective messaging services to engage in the agreed-upon business process in accordance with the constraints defined in the TPA.

ebXML message service

The ebXML *Technical Architecture Specification* defines an ebXML *message service* in order to provide a standard way to exchange business messages among ebXML trading partners. Conceptually, the ebXML messaging service consists of (1) an abstract service interface, (2) a messaging service layer, and (3) transport services. Figure 6.8 shows the ebXML message service functional architecture and its relationship to ebXML applications and transport services [33].

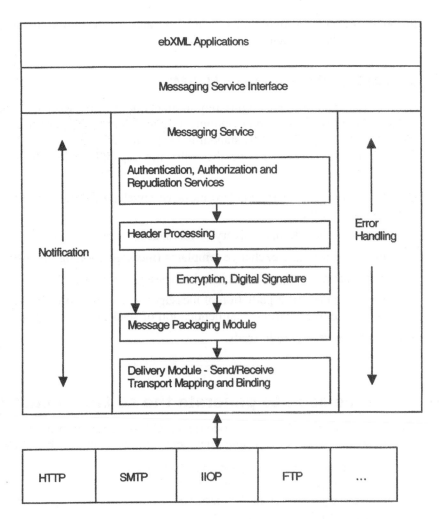

Figure 6.8   *ebXML message service functional architecture.*

The ebXML message service permits use of a variety of protocols for the transport service, including HTTP and Internet inter-orb protocol (IIOP). While HTTP is the most commonly used protocol for HTML applications, use of IIOP is well suited for applications where XML is used in place of a CORBA IDL.

UN/CEFACT and OASIS have announced plans to integrate the simple object access protocol (SOAP) into the ebXML message service. SOAP is a lightweight XML-based protocol for exchange of information in a decentralized environment. SOAP consists of three parts: an envelope that defines a framework for describing what is in a message and how to process it; a set of encoding rules for expressing instances of application-defined datatypes; and a convention for representing remote procedure call and responses [34].

Java API for XML messaging (JAXM)

In order to support the messaging requirements of ebXML, work has begun in the Java Community Process on development of an API for XML messaging, based on the OASIS/CEFACT ebXML standards [35]. The Java API for XML messaging (JAXM) is intended to provide the following capabilities for ebXML business transactions:

- Support for an industry standard message envelope and headers for routing of message content;
- Support for the reliable delivery of messages;
- Support for message exchange templates (message choreographies);
- Support for a variety of data types in message payloads;
- Support for the non-repudiation of messages – privacy and integrity of communications between parties – authentication of senders of messages;
- Support for secure audit trails.

6.6 XML4J source code to generate the so.xml document

This section contains the source code for an XML4J program to create and print out the so.xml service order example document referenced in the above text.

```
import com.ibm.xml.parser.TXDocument;
import org.W3C.dom.Document;
import org.W3C.dom.Element;
import org.W3C.dom.Text;
import java.io.PrintWriter;

public class MakeServiceOrderDoc {
  public static void main(String[] argv) {
    try {

      //create a Document object
      Document so = (Document)Class.forName
        ("com.ibm.xml.parser.TXDocument")
          .newInstance();

      //Make the service order element the root
      Element root = so.createElement("ServiceOrder");
```

```
//Add date attribute to service order
root.setAttribute("orderDate", "28-02-2001");

//Add service address element to service order
Element elem1 =
  so.createElement("ServiceAddress");
root.appendChild(elem1);

//Add business address element to service order
Element elem2 =
  so.createElement("BusinessAddress");
root.appendChild(elem2);

//Add type of service element to service order
Element elem3 = so.createElement("TypeOfService");
root.appendChild(elem3);

//Add name element to service address
Element elem4 = so.createElement("name");
elem4.appendChild
  (so.createTextNode("Arthur Smith"));
elem1.appendChild(elem4);

//Add street element to service address
Element elem5 = so.createElement("street");
elem5.appendChild
  (so.createTextNode("100 Main Street"));
elem1.appendChild(elem5);

//Add city element to service address
Element elem6 = so.createElement("city");
elem6.appendChild
  (so.createTextNode("Davenport"));
elem1.appendChild(elem6);

//Add state element to service address
Element elem7 = so.createElement("state");
elem7.appendChild(so.createTextNode("IA"));
elem1.appendChild(elem7);

//Add zip code element to service address
Element elem8 = so.createElement("zip");
elem8.appendChild(so.createTextNode("52806"));
elem1.appendChild(elem8);
```

```
//Add name element to business address
Element elem9 = so.createElement("name");
elem9.appendChild
  (so.createTextNode("Jane Smith"));
elem2.appendChild(elem9);

//Add street element to business address
Element elem10 = so.createElement("street");
elem10.appendChild(so.createTextNode("400 Jones
  Street"));
elem2.appendChild(elem10);

//Add city element to business address
Element elem11 = so.createElement("city");
elem11.appendChild
  (so.createTextNode("Davenport"));
elem2.appendChild(elem11);

//Add state element to business address
Element elem12 = so.createElement("state");
elem12.appendChild(so.createTextNode("IA"));
elem2.appendChild(elem12);

//Add zip code element to business address
Element elem13 = so.createElement("zip");
elem13.appendChild(so.createTextNode("52806"));
elem2.appendChild(elem13);

//Add service category element to type of service
Element elem14 =
  so.createElement("ServiceCategory");
elem14.appendChild(so.createTextNode("adsl"));
elem3.appendChild(elem14);

//Add service level element to type of service
Element elem15 = so.createElement("ServiceLevel");
elem15.appendChild
  (so.createTextNode("premium"));
elem3.appendChild(elem15);

//Add bandwidth element to type of service
Element elem16 = so.createElement("bandwidth");
elem16.appendChild(so.createTextNode("1000"));
elem3.appendChild(elem16);
```

```
        //append the root element to the document
        so.appendChild(root);

        //display the XML document
        ((TXDocument)so).setVersion("1.0");
        ((TXDocument)so).printWithFormat(new PrintWriter
            (System.out));
    } catch (Exception e) {
    e.printStackTrace();
    }
  }
}
```

References

1. RETS Working Group Home Page, http://www.rets-wg.org/.

2. Chemical markup language, http://www.xml-cml.org.

3. Standards Committee T1, T1M1 – Internetwork operations, administration, maintenance and provisioning, http://www.t1.org/t1m1/t1m1.htm. The tML framework document (work in progress) may be downloaded from ftp://ftp.t1.org/pub/t1m1/new-t1m1.0/1m100020.doc.

4. Bray T Paoli J, Sperberg-McQueen CM, Maler E, editors. Extensible markup language (XML) 1.0. Second Edition. W3C Recommendation, 6 October 2000. http://www.w3.org/TR/2000/REC-xml-20001006.

5. Bos B, Wium Lie H, Lilley C, Jacobs I, editors. Cascading style sheets, level 2, CSS2 specification, W3C Recommendation, 12 May 1998. http://www.w3.org/TR/1998/REC-CSS2-19980512.

6. Adler S, Berglund A, Caruso J, Deach S, Grasso P, Gutentag E, Milowski A, Parnell S, Richman J, Zilles S, editors. Extensible style sheet language (XSL) version 1.0. W3C Candidate Recommendation, 21 November 2000 (work in progress). http://www.w3.org/TR/2000/CR-xsl-20001121/.

7. Clark J, editor. XSL transformations (XSLT) version 1.0. W3C Recommendation, 16 November 1999. http://www.W3C.org/TR/1999/REC-xslt-19991116.

8. For more information on WAP, see http://www.wapforum.org/faqs/index.htm.

9. WAP specifications are located at http://www.wapforum.org/what/technical.htm.

10. Mahmoud QH. WAP for Java developers: develop WAP applications with Java servlets and JavaServer pages. JavaWorld, June 2000.

11. Wood L, Apparao V, Byrne S, Champion M, Isaacs S, Jacobs I, Le Hors A, Nicol G, Robie J, Sutor R, Wilson C, editors. Document object model (DOM) level 1 specification version 1.0. W3C Recommendation, 1 October 1998. http://www.w3.org/TR/1998/REC-DOM-Level-1-19981001.

12. Le Hors A, Le Hegaret P, Wood L, Nicol G, Robie J, Champion M, Byrne S, editors.

Document object model (DOM) level 2 core specification version 1.0. W3C Recommendation, 13 November 2000. http://www.w3.org/TR/2000/REC-DOM-Level-2-Core-20001113.

13. Bray T, Hollander D, Layman A. Namespaces in XML. W3C Recommendation, 14 January 1999. http://www.w3.org/TR/1999/REC-xml-names-19990114.

14. Lassila O, Swick RR. Resource description framework (RDF) model and syntax specification. W3C Recommendation, 22 February 1999. http://www.w3.org/TR/1999/REC-rdf-syntax-19990222.

15. Fallside DC. XML schema part 0: primer. W3C Recommendation, 2 May 2001; http://www.w3.org/TR/2001/REC-xmlschema-0-20010502/primer.html.

16. Thompson HS, Beech D, Maloney M, Mendelsohn N. XML schema part 1: structures. W3C Recommendation, 2 May 2001; http://www.w3.org/TR/2001/REC-xmlschema-1-200010502/

17. Viron PB, Malhotra A. XML schema part 2: datatypes. W3C Recommendation, 2 May 2001; http://www.w3.org/TR/2001/REC-xmlschema-2-200010502/.

18. The SAX API can be found at http://www.megginson.com/SAX/index.html.

19. Maruyama H, Tamura K, Uramoto N. XML and Java: developing web applications. Reading, MA: Addison Wesley, 1999. This book references version 2.0 of XML4J; the most current version may be downloaded from http://alphaworks.ibm.com/tech/xml4j?open&l=xmlin,t=gr,p=xml4j2001.

20. Davidson JD, et al, Java API for XML parsing, version 1.0. March 2, 2000. http://java.sun.com/aboutJava/communityprocess/final/jsr005/index.html.

21. Apache XML project, http://xml.apache.org/. IBM was a major contributor to the Apache Xerces Java code base, and there are many similarities between XML4J and Xerces. However, IBM has continued to develop XML4J independently of the Apache project as well.

22. Armstrong E. Code fast, run fast with XML data binding. http://java.sun.com/xml/docs/binding/DataBinding.html.

23. ITU-T M.3010, Principles for a telecommunications management network, 1996.

24. Raman LG, Fundamentals of telecommunications network management. Piscataway, NJ: IEEE Press, 1999, pp. 12–17, 56–7.

25. ITU-T Recommendation X.710, Common management information service definition, 1997; ITU-T Recommendation X.711, information technology – open systems interconnection - common management information protocol specification – part 1, 1997.

26. ITU-T X.722, Information technology - open systems interconnection - structure of management information: guidelines for the definition of managed objects, 1992; ITU-T X.680-X.683, Open systems interconnection - specification of abstract notation one (ASN.1), parts 1–4, 1996.

27. Case J, Fedor M, Schoffstall M, Davin J. A simple network management protocol, IETF RFC 1157, May 1990.

28. Object management group common object request broker architecture and specification, version 2.0, 1995.

29. GR-831-CORE. Operations application messages: language for operations application messages. Telcordia November 1996;1.

30. United Nations Centre for Trade Facilitation and Electronic Business, http://www.unece.org/cefact/.

31. Organization for the Advancement of Structured Information Standards, http://www.oasis-open.org/.

32. ebXML Technical Architectural Team. ebXML technical architectural specification, v1.0.4, 16 February 2001. http://www.ebxml.org/specs/ebTA.pdf.

33. ibid, p. 29.

34. Box D, Ehnebuske D, Kakivaya G, Layman A, Mendelsohn N, Nielsen HF, Thatte S, Winer D. Simple object access protocol (SOAP) 1.1. W3C Note, 8 May 2000 (work in progress). http://www.w3.org/TR/2000/NOTE-SOAP-20000508.

35. Kassem N. JSR000067, Java APIs for XML Messaging 1.0, June 26, 2000 (work in progress). http://java.sun.com/aboutJava/communityprocess/jsr/jsr_067_jaxm.html.

Glossary of terms

Accounting Management	TMN management functional area. Provides mechanisms for billing customers for using network resources.
AEG	Application Expert Group; in the Java Community Process, a group that addresses application-level issues.
AIN	Advanced Intelligent Network. A set of Bellcore-developed specifications for an equipment-independent network architecture.
ANSI	American National Standards Institute. A private organization that administers and coordinates the US voluntary standardization and conformity assessment system.
API	Application Programming Interface. A set of software calls or language bindings that enable applications to access system or network services in a standard and reusable fashion.
Applet	Portable unit of Java code that does not have a main() method. References to applets are typically embedded in HTML code with an ⟨APPLET⟩ tag.
ASN.1	Abstract Syntax Notation One. A notation, defined in ITU-T X.208, which provides a level of abstraction similar to that provided by higher level programming languages for interchanging information between management systems and managed entities.
ATIS	Alliance for Telecommunications Industry Solutions. A North American standards body that is leading the development of telecommunications standards, operating procedures, and guidelines through its sponsored committees and fora.
ATM	(1) Asynchronous Transfer Mode. A data transfer technology based on fixed-size 53-byte cells. (2) Automated Teller Machine.
BCP	Basic Call Process.
BDK	Beans Development Kit. A set of Java tools for developing JavaBeans.
CA	Call Agent.
Card	A single user interaction in WML.
CDATA	A type of XML markup used to escape blocks of data containing characters that would otherwise be treated as markup.
CEFACT	Centre for Trade Facilitation and Electronic Business. The United Nations body whose mandate covers worldwide policy and technical development in the area of trade facilitation and electronic business.

CIC	Circuit Identification Code. A code used to identify individual trunk circuits in the SS7 network architecture.
CMIP	Common Management Information Protocol. TMN-defined protocol used for CMISE.
CMISE	Common Management Information Service Element. TMN-defined application layer service used for network management.
COBOL	Common Business Oriented Language. An early programming language used primarily for business applications.
Component	A specific operation requested by an application in the SS7 network architecture.
Configuration Management	TMN functional area. Deals with provisioning of the equipment in the network element, adding, deleting or modifying circuits, configuring multiple network elements in a topology to form a network, etc.
CORBA	Common Object Request Broker Architecture. A distributed object architecture, developed and standardized by the Object Management Group (OMG).
CPU	Central Processing Unit. The primary processor in a computer.
CSS	Cascading Style Sheets. A style sheet language that enables document creators to attach style specifications to structured HTML and XML documents.
CUIS	Call User Interaction Service. A call specialization of GUIS allowing intelligent voice recognition for intelligent peripheral and voicemail systems.
DCOM	Distributed Component Object Model. The distributed version of Microsoft's Component Object Model (COM) which allows network-based component interaction.
DOM	Document Object Model. A W3C standard which defines the structure of an XML document.
DTD	Document Type Definition. An entity used for document validation in XML.
DTMF	Dual-Tone Multifrequency. A tone signaling system used for telephony digit dialing.
ebXML	Electronic Business XML. ebXML is an effort to standardize electronic business transactions and is jointly sponsored by the United Nations Centre for Trade Facilitation and Electronic Business (UN/CEFACT) and the Organization for the Advancement of Structured Information Standards (OASIS).
EML	Element Management Layer. The layer in the Telecommunications Management Network architecture which performs element management. The process of configuring, monitoring and controlling any network element can be partitioned into this layer.
EJB	Enterprise JavaBeans. Java-based software components which provide server-side business logic or middleware functions.
Entity Bean	EJBs which encapsulate the data tier of an n-tier application. Entity beans typically map to a row of a table in a relational database.
ESCON	Enterprise Systems Connection. A storage area networking protocol, developed by IBM for interconnecting mainframe computers and storage devices.
Fault Management	TMN functional area. Fault management consists of monitoring the network elements for any faults, alarms or events.
FCAPS	Acronym for the full set of TMN functional areas: Fault, Configuration, Accounting, Performance, and Security.

FSM	Finite State Machine. A set of states and state transitions used to represent a software function.
GK	Gatekeeper. A component in the H.323 architecture which provides address translation, admission control, bandwidth control, and zone management.
GCCS	Generic Call Control Service (in Parlay). A call control service suitable for ISUP, H.323, INAP, Advanced IN (AIN), VoIP and CTI call domains. This service can be used for either the first party (terminal) or third party (switch) cases.
GDMO	Guidelines for the Definition of Managed Objects. A notion, described in ITU-T X.722, which defines keywords structured in a template format.
GMS	Generic Messaging Service. A messaging service providing the ability to send, receive, translate and manage multimedia messages and mailboxes.
GSM	Global System for Mobile Communications. The European standard for digital networks, which guarantees compatibility of wireless devices.
GUI	Graphical User Interface. A user interface that is graphically based, rather than text-based.
GUIS	Generic User Interaction Service. A skeleton service, currently only extended by the Call User Interaction Service.
HTML	Hypertext Markup Language. HTML is the "lingua franca" for publishing hypertext on the World Wide Web.
HTTP	Hypertext Transport Protocol. The protocol used by the World Wide Web for transport of HTML documents.
H.323	ITU-T standard for packet-based multimedia communications systems.
IDE	Integrated Development Environment. A set of tools for compiling, building, editing, browsing, and debugging software in an integrated and modular fashion.
IDL	Interface Definition Language. A language used to define the interface to objects in CORBA, to determine the operations that may be performed and the input and output parameters.
IETF	Internet Engineering Task Force. An international community of designers, operators, and researchers concerned with the evolution and operation of the Internet.
IIOP	Internet Inter-ORB Protocol. The standard protocol used to specify target object, operation, and input/output parameters between object request brokers (ORBs) in CORBA.
IN	Intelligent Network. A Bellcore-developed equipment-independent telecommunications network architecture that moves functionality out of the switching equipment and into a distributed intelligent network.
INAP	Intelligent Network Application Part. Protocols used for switch-to-SCP, SCP-to-SDP, and SCP-to-IP communications in the IN architecture.
IP	1) Internet Protocol. The IETF-defined protocol used to send data from one computer to another on the Internet. 2) Intelligent Peripheral. A component of the IN architecture which supports specialized resource functions.
IS41	A TIA/EIA standard for Wireless Intelligent Networks which implements intersystem operations by defining data messages and procedures for using them between logical network elements.
ISUP	Integrated Services Digital Network User Part. SS7 protocol used to set up, test, maintain, and tear down circuits.

ITU	International Telecommunication Union. A specialized agency of the United Nations that is responsible for dealing with telecommunications issues.
ITU-T	International Telecommunication Union – Telecommunication Standardization Sector. A sector of the ITU that is responsible for telecommunications standardization.
J2EE	Java 2 Platform, Enterprise Edition. A Java 2 platform intended for developing multi-tiered thin-client applications using servlets and EJBs.
JAIN	Java APIs for Integrated Networks. A set of integrated network APIs for the Java platform that provides a framework to build and integrate solutions and services spanning packet, wireless, and PSTN networks.
JAR	Java Archive. File format used to bundle multiple files into a single archive file. JAR files use the ZIP format.
JAXM	Java API for XML Messaging. An industry standard message envelope and headers for routing of XML message content.
JAXP	Java API for XML Parsing. An API developed as part of the Java Community Process for parsing and manipulating XML documents.
JCAT	Java Coordination and Transactions. An extension package to JCC which supports coordination and transaction-related methods.
JCC	Java Call Control. The JAIN API which supports the basic call model for call processing and control.
JCP	(1) Java Community Process. The formal process for developing or revising Java technology specifications. (2) Java Call Processing.
JDBC	Java Database Connectivity. JDBC provides a Standard Query Language (SQL) database interface, allowing access to a wide variety of relational databases.
JDK	Java Developers' Kit. A set of tools and classes for developing Java applications.
JFC	Java Foundation Classes. A set of classes added to the Java 2 platform which extend the functionality of the java.awt classes by adding a comprehensive set of GUI class libraries.
JMS	Java Message Service. An API for providing reliable, asynchronous messaging between components in a distributed computing environment.
JMX	Java Management Extensions. Java API for distributed, web-based management solutions.
JNDI	Java Naming and Directory Interface. An API which provides a common interface to network directory and naming services.
JNI	Java Native Interface. An API which provides an interface to code written in languages other than Java.
JSCE	Java Service Creation Environment. In the JAIN architecture, the environment where new services are created.
JSLEE	Java Service Logic Execution Environment. In the JAIN architecture, the environment in which service logic is executed.
JSP	Java Server Pages. Java components which allow HTML- or XML-based user interfaces to be interactively updated.
JSR	Java Specification Request. The document submitted to the Process Management Office by one or more members of the Java Community Process to propose the development of a new specification or significant revision to an existing specification.

JTAPI	Java Telephony API. A portable, object-oriented interface for Java-based computer telephony applications.
JTS	Java Transaction Service. The JTS specifies the implementation of a transaction manager which supports the Java Transaction API (JTA).
JVM	Java Virtual Machine. A component used to interpret Java bytecode at runtime.
LAN	Local Area Network. A group of computers and associated devices that share a common communications line and processor or server.
Logging	Creating a persistent record of system events, such as faults or configuration changes.
MAN	Metropolitan Area Network. A network that connects users with computer resources in a geographical area larger than a LAN, but smaller than a WAN, such as a city.
MAP	Mobile Application Part. A protocol used to support wireless services in the IN architecture.
Megaco	Protocol used between elements of a physically decomposed multimedia gateway, defined in RFC3015.
MG	Media Gateway. A media gateway converts media provided in one type of network to the format required in another type of network.
MGCP	Media Gateway Control Protocol. A protocol used for call/connection setup between the media gateway (MG) and the media gateway controller in a distributed architecture.
MIB	Management Information Base. A repository of managed objects and their properties.
MIDL	Microsoft IDL. An IDL used to specify COM and DCOM objects and interfaces.
MTP	Message Transfer Part. A protocol used as part of the SS7 architecture to provide transport of routing, network configuration, and management messages.
Namespace	A collection of names, identified by a URI, which are used in XML documents as element types and attribute names.
NEL	Network Element Layer. The layer in the Telecommunications Management Network architecture which comprises network elements. A network element can be a workstation, router, ATM switch, Digital cross connect, Add-Drop Multiplexor or any other network connected device.
NIST	National Institute for Standards and Technology. An agency of the US Commerce Department that works with industry to develop and apply technology, measurements, and standards.
NML	Network Management Layer. The layer in the Telecommunications Management Network architecture which performs network management. Network management provides an overall network view and is able to perform operations within or across the complete breadth of the network.
NOC	Network Operations Center. A center where network management is performed by a carrier or service provider. Acts as a focal point for performing network-wide operations such as provisioning, monitoring the health of the network and statistical data collection.
OAM	Operations, Administration and Maintenance. A set of functions for the operation and maintenance of a telecommunications system, typically performed by a management system.

OASIS	Organization for the Advancement of Structured Information Standards. An international consortium that advances electronic business by promoting open, collaborative development of interoperability specifications.
ODBC	Open Database Connectivity. A Microsoft database access API that provides a level of abstraction from proprietary database interfaces.
OMG	Object Management Group. A consortium formed to provide a solution for implementing portable software components. Developers of the CORBA specifications.
ORB	Object Request Broker. A mechanism which allows distributed objects to interact with one another in CORBA.
Parlay	A set of APIs external to the secure network operator space, developed by the Parlay Group.
PBX	Private Branch Exchange. A customer-premise-located switching device which enables calls to be connected within the enterprise, or between an enterprise user and the public network.
PC	Personal Computer. A small computing unit intended for personal use.
PEG	Protocols Expert Group. A group within the JAIN community process focused on development of protocol APIs.
Performance Management	TMN functional area. Deals with collection of data about the network in order to derive usage statistics, load information, etc. in order to efficiently plan for expansion of the network or monitor for patterns in the network that may need increased attention for failures.
PSTN	Public Switched Telecommunications Network. The public telephony network.
Q Interface	A "vertical" interface between an operations system (OS) and a network element, or between two levels of an OS within the same TMN.
QoS	Quality of Service. An objective measure of service level, including parameters such as bandwidth, data loss, latency, and jitter.
Rate Monotonic Scheduling	A scheduling algorithm in which task priority is assigned in the order of decreasing execution frequency. Tasks that execute most frequently are assigned the highest priority, and tasks that execute least often are assigned the lowest execution priority.
RI	Reference Implementation. The prototype or "proof of concept" implementation of a specification in the Java Community Process.
RMI	Remote Method Invocation. RMI enables distributed Java-to-Java applications in which the methods of remote Java objects can be invoked from other Java virtual machines on different hosts.
RPG	Report Program Generator. A report generating program, originally used in DEC and IBM minicomputers, which eventually evolved into a fully procedural programming language.
RTP	Realtime Transport Protocol. A protocol for providing end-to-end network transport of real-time services such as voice and video.
RTCP	Realtime Transport Control Protocol.. A control protocol for RTP which provides monitoring, control and identification functions.
RTSJ	Real Time Specification for Java. A specification for adding real-time capabilities to the Java programming language, developed by the Java Community Process.
SAX	Simple API for XML. An event-based API for XML used to parse XML documents.

SCE	Service Creation Environment. The framework within which service control software is developed in the IN architecture.
Scheduling	(1) Enabling command execution at specified time intervals, or (2) assigning execution priorities to threads.
Schema	An XML document consisting of a set of components used for document validation.
SCP	Service Control Point. An entity which provides service logic execution capability in the IN architecture.
SCCP	Signaling Connection Control Part. An SS7 protocol which provides both connection-oriented and connectionless transport services.
SCTP	Stream Control Transport Protocol. A reliable transport protocol designed to transport PSTN signaling messages over IP networks.
SDK	Software Developers' Kit. The software that implements the Java 2 platform.
SDP	Service Data Point. A component which provides subscriber data storage and access capability in the IN architecture.
Security Management	TMN functional area. Security management deals with issues such as user permissions, user access audits, password authentication, etc. It ensures that the network is secure such that unwanted elements cannot gain access through the management systems.
Servlet	Java-based components that provide functions similar to CGI scripts on the server and act as an interface between client requests and system services.
Session Bean	Session beans are EJBs which implement the actual business logic of an application.
SGML	Standard Generalized Markup Language. An ISO standard for how to specify a markup language or tag set, defined in ISO 8879:1986(E).
SIB	Service Independent Building Block. Global functional units used for service creation in the IN architecture.
SIP	Session Initiation Protocol. A text-based, transport-independent protocol that enables the transport of multimedia traffic over an IP network.
SLEE	Service Logic Execution Environment. In the IN architecture, the environment in which service logic executes.
SLP	Service Location Protocol. An intradomain protocol used for gateway location discovery.
SML	Service Management Layer. The layer in the Telecommunications Management Network architecture which performs service management. Service management deals with the processes required to monitor, command and control the actual services delivered by the network elements.
SNMP	Simple Network Management Protocol. IETF-defined protocol used for Internet network management.
SOAP	Simple Object Access Protocol. A lightweight XML-based protocol for exchange of information in a decentralized environment.
SP	Signaling Point A component which appears as a local exchange to the user and provides an interface to the SS7 network.
SPC	Signaling Point Code. A unique point code used to identify each endpoint and STP in the SS7 network.
SQL	Structured Query Language. A standard programming language for updating and retrieving data from a database. Although SQL is an ANSI/ISO standard, many database products support SQL with proprietary extensions.

SS7	Signaling System No. 7. An ITU-T developed standard for common channel signaling.
SSP	Service Switching Point A switch which provides access to IN capabilities.
STP	Signal Transfer Point. A component in the IN architecture which provides signaling and routing capability.
Swing	Java 2 GUI classes which provide pluggable look and feel.
T1M1	The Internetwork Operations, Administration, Maintenance, and Provisioning subcommittee of Committee T1. Committee T1 - Telecommunications is a US standards group, sponsored by ATIS and accredited by ANSI.
TAPI	Telephony API. An API, developed by Microsoft, which enables voice calls to be set up and completed using computers connected to the Internet.
TCA	Threshold Crossing Alert. A network management event notification indicating that some pre-determined threshold value has been exceeded.
TCAP	Transaction Capabilities Application Part. A transaction-oriented protocol, typically used between a switch and a database in an SS7 environment.
TCK	Technology Compatibility Kit. A suite of tests that a vendor must run and pass in order to claim JAIN Compliance.
TCP/IP	Transport Control Protocol/Internet Protocol. The basic protocol of the Internet. The TCP layer manages the assembly of data into packets for transport over the Internet. The IP layer handles the address part of each packet.
TL1	Transaction Language 1. An ASCII-based man/machine language used for network management.
TMN	Telecommunications Management Network. An architecture for telecommunications network management, developed by the ITU-T.
TPA	Trading Partner Agreement. An agreement among business partners on how to conduct ebXML-based business transactions.
Transaction	A dialog between two applications in the SS7 network architecture.
UML	Unified Modeling Language. UML is a language for specifying, visualizing, constructing, and documenting the artifacts of software systems. UML has been released as an open standard by the OMG.
URI	Uniform Resource Identifier. Short strings that identify resources on the Web.
URL	Uniform Resource Locator. Internet addresses; the set of URIs that have explicit instructions on how to access the resource on the Internet.
VOIP	Voice Over IP. A network architecture which supports voice telephony over an IP packet network.
VPN	Virtual Private Network. A private data network which makes use of the public telecommunications infrastructure. It maintains privacy through the use of a tunneling protocol and security procedures.
W3C	World Wide Web Consortium. An international consortium of companies and academic institutions tasked with developing open standards for Internet Web applications.
WAN	Wide Area Network. A geographically dispersed telecommunications network.
WAP	Wireless Application Protocol. A protocol used for content presentation on a wireless terminal.
WML	Wireless Markup Language. An XML-based markup language designed to be used with Wireless Application Protocol (WAP).

WORA	Write Once, Run Anywhere. Brief statement of Java's goal of total platform independence.
WWW	World Wide Web. The universe of network-accessible information; an embodiment of human knowledge.
X Interface	A "horizontal" interface between two peer OS layers in different TMNs.
XML	Extensible Markup Language. A language for describing markup languages, developed and standardized by the W3C.
XML4J	XML for Java. A tool developed by IBM Corporation for processing XML documents
XSL	Extensible Stylesheet Language. A language for expressing style sheets in XML.
XSLT	XSL Transformations. The process of constructing a result tree in XML using XSL.

Index

Printed and bound in the UK by
CPI Antony Rowe, Eastbourne

Printed and bound by CPI Group (UK) Ltd, Croydon, CR0 4YY

27/10/2024

14580217-0001